STANFORD BOOKS IN

World Politics

STANFORD BOOKS IN WORLD POLITICS

Graham H. Stuart, *Editor*

Herbert Hoover's
Latin-American Policy

Herbert Hoover's Latin-American Policy

ALEXANDER DeCONDE

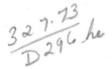
STANFORD UNIVERSITY PRESS
STANFORD, CALIFORNIA
LONDON : GEOFFREY CUMBERLEGE, OXFORD UNIVERSITY PRESS

STANFORD UNIVERSITY PRESS, STANFORD, CALIFORNIA
LONDON: GEOFFREY CUMBERLEGE, OXFORD UNIVERSITY PRESS

THE BAKER AND TAYLOR COMPANY, 55 FIFTH AVENUE, NEW YORK 3
HENRY M. SNYDER & COMPANY, 440 FOURTH AVENUE, NEW YORK 16
W. S. HALL & COMPANY, 457 MADISON AVENUE, NEW YORK 22

TO MY MOTHER

FOREWORD

The final verdict of history on human events is never handed down by contemporaneous opinion. It is only when the various influences and factors, often secret or overlooked at the time, are given adequate consideration that a true evaluation is possible.

Former President Herbert Hoover has suffered particularly from hasty generalizations based upon inadequate and often biased information. Today, although two decades have passed since his presidency, a much more objective view of his achievements is possible.

This study by Dr. Alexander DeConde affords a striking illustration of the revised evaluation based upon a complete background. With the publication of the Foreign Relations volumes and with access to the Hoover papers, Dr. DeConde has been able to present President Hoover's policy toward Latin America in its proper environment. Beginning with the good-will mission before inauguration, President Hoover's efforts to maintain peace and good will in the Americas are effectively portrayed. It was essentially a nonpartisan policy based upon frank and friendly co-operation and, although the "good-neighbor" policy is generally associated with the name of Franklin D. Roosevelt, the real beginning was made both in name and deed by Herbert Hoover. A positive policy of nonintervention was his purpose, and the withdrawal of Marines from Nicaragua and Haiti proved it. He favored the peaceful settlement of disputes and he was instrumental in ending the Tacna-Arica dispute which had plagued South America for over half a century.

Herbert Hoover himself expressed the fundamental principle of his policy when he declared that one of his greatest satisfactions as President was the opportunity which it gave him to show his sympathy and interest in the well-being of our sister republics. This carefully documented and well-written study by Dr. DeConde indicates that he succeeded.

GRAHAM H. STUART

STANFORD UNIVERSITY
STANFORD, CALIFORNIA
December 1, 1949

PREFACE

"We shall use words to convey our meaning, not to hide it."
—HERBERT HOOVER, 1928

"Our relations with Latin America are, above all, not in any way partisan."
—UNDERSECRETARY OF STATE WILLIAM R. CASTLE, JR., 1931

Herbert Hoover's Latin-American policy was not an isolated entity; it was an integral part of the larger foreign policy of his administration. In this study the subject is treated as a unit, but always with the knowledge that it was a vital part of a larger and more important whole. The four years of Hoover's administration have been largely neglected or have been given scant attention by historians in treating the historical evolution of our Latin-American policy. Only within the past few years have a few writers gone back to the Hoover administration and to the preceding years in an effort to find the beginnings of the "good-neighbor" policy.

As there is no full treatment of the Latin-American policies of the Hoover administration available, an attempt is here made to trace their history. Particular emphasis is placed on the changes in inter-American relations wrought by the Hoover policies, noting at the same time how these policies differed from or compared with those of Hoover's predecessors. Wherever possible, some indication is given as to how opinion, both in the United States and south of the border, reacted to these policies.

In making an evaluation of the Latin-American policy of the Hoover administration, which was probably the least criticized and the least publicized of all of the Hoover policies, several factors must be kept in mind. Although Hoover was perhaps more concerned with inter-American relations than was any other preceding President, these relations occupied a relatively minor place in government policy in the last two years of his administration. In those years Hoover's main efforts were devoted to internal affairs. From October 1929 to his last day in office he struggled with the nightmare of an economic depression and its concomitant effect on foreign relations. In foreign affairs, inter-American relations were overshadowed by the problems of Europe and the Far East, where Hoover and his contemporaries were deeply involved in the problems of world disarmament, war debts, reparations, and the activities of the Mikado's armies in Manchuria.

Nevertheless, the necessity of cultivating a friendly policy with Latin America was evident to Hoover. His efforts followed his ideal of the "good neighbor," and produced dividends during his administration and later. Not until impending world conflict threatened the Western Hemisphere and brought about a marriage of necessity between the Americas was greater significance attached to the "good-neighbor" concept as it was practiced by the Franklin D. Roosevelt administration. Consequently this policy of consolidating relations with the southern nations received greater publicity, and became firmly associated in the minds of many with the Roosevelt regime. Roosevelt held the reins of government for twelve uninterrupted years, whereas Hoover was in office for only four years. Roosevelt guided the country's foreign policy through a world war that made the American people conscious of foreign affairs, while Hoover was a depression President who had to conduct the nation's foreign relations when isolationism waxed strongest in the United States. It is perhaps not strange that the importance of the Hoover policies has been for the most part overlooked.

The author is indebted to many persons for aid and assistance in the preparation of this volume, though any errors of fact or interpretation are his own. It is with particular pleasure that he acknowledges the constructive advice and suggestions of Thomas A. Bailey, Miss Suda L. Bane, John J. Johnson, Edgar E. Robinson, Graham H. Stuart, Harry W. Nerhood, and Paul S. Smith. The staff of the Hoover Library was especially helpful and extended many courtesies beyond mere routine. The labor and patience of the writer's wife, Jeanne Seeger DeConde, are reflected in every page.

ALEXANDER DeCONDE

WHITTIER COLLEGE
WHITTIER, CALIFORNIA
September 1949

CONTENTS

Herbert Hoover's
Latin-American Policy

CHAPTER I

BACKGROUNDS, 1920–1928

"The person and property of a citizen are a part of the general domain of the nation, even when abroad [and] there is a distinct and binding obligation on the part of self-respecting governments to afford protection to the persons and property of their citizens, wherever they may be."   —PRESIDENT CALVIN COOLIDGE, 1927

The Pan-Americanism of President Woodrow Wilson was a brand of idealism that evolved into a kind of moral meddling, resulting in a series of interventions in the internal affairs of several Caribbean powers. In spite of Wilson's professed friendship for Latin America and his distaste for "dollar diplomacy," the practicalities of statecraft led him to undertake more armed interventions in Latin America than any of his predecessors.[1] Nevertheless, he has been credited with inspiring a new Latin-American policy for the United States.[2] This new policy, taken over by Hughes, Hoover, and Stimson, blossomed forth into the "good-neighbor" policy that many Americans, north and south, have associated with the Franklin D. Roosevelt administration.

It was in relation to the turbulent and often bloody affairs of Mexico that Wilson promulgated a new principle, which then was generally imposed on the Latin-American policy of the United States and continued by succeeding administrations until repudiated by Hoover. Wilson obdurately refused to recognize the government of Victoriano Huerta, which came to power in Mexico in February 1913, after deposing the regime of the reforming idealist, Francisco Madero. As a prisoner of Huerta, Madero was murdered on February 23, 1913, under circumstances that made Huerta seem responsible for the

[1] Cf. Thomas A. Bailey, *A Diplomatic History of the American People*, 2d ed., p. 596; Charles E. Chapman, *Republican Hispanic America*, p. 150.

[2] See his address of October 27, 1913, "A New Latin-American Policy," in Ray S. Baker and William E. Dodd, eds., *The Public Papers of Woodrow Wilson*, I, 64–69.

3

treacherous act. This affair appeared especially villainous, since Huerta had sworn a personal responsibility for the life of Madero.[3]

In the wake of these events, and shortly after he was inaugurated, President Wilson on March 11, 1913, made a "Declaration of Policy with Regard to Latin America."[4] This was sent to United States diplomatic posts throughout the southern continent. In essence, it set up the United States as a self-appointed judge over the internal conflicts of states claiming and exercising the attributes of sovereignty. Wilson expressed the doctrine that governments established by force in violation of their country's constitution, and against the will of the people, would not be recognized or receive support from the United States. He maintained that "co-operation is possible only when supported at every turn by the orderly processes of just government based upon law, not upon arbitrary or irregular force."

This was a marked departure from the traditional practice of international law, as adhered to by most countries of the world. To many of the southern republics this doctrine seemed nothing more than another form of intervention in their domestic affairs,[5] since recognition was usually based upon *de facto* control and not upon *de jure* succession, as Wilson wished to have it.[6]

When the Republican "dynasty" resumed control in 1921 under the apostle of "normalcy," President Warren G. Harding, Wilson's Latin-American policy, along with the League of Nations problem, was left on the new administration's doorstep. The problem of the League was shelved, but the Latin-American affairs of the nation were given the guidance of the prominent statesman, Charles Evans Hughes, whom Harding chose as his Secretary of State. Hughes directed the foreign policies of the United States for four years, partly under Harding and partly under the administration of Calvin Coolidge.

Secretary Hughes carried on many of Wilson's Latin-American policies, chief of which was the recognition policy. He also attempted to remove the basis for the hackneyed epithet, "Yankee imperialism," and sought to apply the salve of understanding and co-operation to

[3] Department of State, *Papers Relating to the Foreign Relations of the United States, 1913*, pp. 731–32 and *passim*. Hereafter cited as *Foreign Relations*. See also *ibid.*, p. 175.

[4] For the text see *ibid.*, p. 7.

[5] See Gaston Nerval, *Autopsy of the Monroe Doctrine*, p. 282.

[6] See Sir John F. Williams, "Recognition," *Transactions of the Grotius Society,* XV (1929), 66–70.

the Latin-American relations of the Washington government. One of the important sources of ill-will between the United States and the Latin countries was to be found in the Dominican Republic. Hughes declared that "no step taken by the government of the United States in Latin America in recent years has given rise to more criticism, and in this instance just criticism, than the military occupation of the Dominican Republic by the armed forces of the United States in 1916 . . . ."[7] As a result of an agreement concluded in 1921 by Hughes, the occupation force of United States Marines was finally withdrawn from the Dominican Republic in September 1924.[8]

Intervention was not eschewed entirely during the early part of Hughes' administration of the nation's foreign affairs, as is evidenced by the landing of United States Marines on the shores of Honduras in March 1924. But here intervention was not unilateral. Through consultation with four of the Central American states, a provisional government was set up and recognized by the United States pending "free and fair elections." At the request of the president of Panama, a small force of Marines was also sent to the Isthmian republic, in October 1925, but remained only a short time.

Under the chairmanship of Secretary of State Hughes a conference on Central American affairs was held in Washington from December 4, 1922, to February 7, 1923. This conference produced fifteen different agreements, including a general treaty of peace and amity, eleven conventions, two protocols, and a declaration by five Central American republics supporting the conservation of peace and solidarity among the signatories.[9]

Another Harding appointee, Herbert Clark Hoover, was also to play a significant part in Latin-American relations. On March 5, 1921, this world-famous food administrator was appointed Secretary of Commerce. Although this office had little to do with government policy in regard to the Hispanic states, it did place Hoover in a position where he was able, both in official and unofficial capacity, to make contact with Latin America and its various peoples. His first public position that had to do specifically with Latin America was the chair-

[7] Quoted in Graham H. Stuart, *Latin America and the United States*, 4th ed., p. 299.

[8] *Foreign Relations, 1924*, I, 643.

[9] Department of State, *Convention for the Establishment of the International Commission of Inquiry (Conference on Central American Affairs)*, p. 284. Hereafter cited as Department of State, *Conference on Central American Affairs*. The Appendix contains the texts of all the agreements in both English and Spanish.

manship of the Inter-American High Commission, to which he was appointed by President Harding on December 20, 1921.[10] The appointment was significant, for until then the Secretary of the Treasury usually headed the commission. The change was interpreted to mean that Hoover was to give his best energies and ability to work that had vital bearing on inter-American commerce and co-operation.

The Inter-American High Commission was organized on the recommendation of the First Pan-American Financial Conference, held in Washington, May 24–29, 1915. Its purpose was to establish a degree of substantial uniformity in the commercial laws and administrative regulations then in effect in the American republics. One of the essential functions of this commission was to assist in bringing about greater stability in the financial relations between the United States and the other republics of the Western Hemisphere. The commission's work was directed by a central executive council, composed of the chairman, vice-chairman, and secretary.[11] Some of the intricacies of inter-American relations were thus familiar to Hoover seven years before he became President.

Early in his governmental career, Hoover took cognizance of the southern continent. Only four days after he became Secretary of Commerce he issued the following statement:

> That the United States is fundamentally interested in Latin America requires no reiteration. In the upbuilding of our relations there is nothing more important than our common interest in trade. The mutual objects must be to increase the standard of living of all our peoples . . . . We have thus a mutual interdependence in the maintenance of our everyday life both North and South . . . . the more we contribute to our joint advance in civilization and the more our intercommerce expands, the more certain is the development of our long established friendships. [12]

Hoover saw the importance of good relations in regard to commerce, and he recognized in Latin America an ever growing market for American goods.

On one occasion, during the administration of Calvin Coolidge, Hoover's ideas on Latin America came into conflict with those of the Department of State. In his remarks on May 2, 1927, at the opening session of the Third Pan-American Commercial Conference, held in

---

[10] *New York Times,* December 21, 1921.

[11] See "Continuing Work of the Financial Conference," *Bulletin of the Pan American Union,* XL (June 1915), 747–48.

[12] Hoover Papers, "Press statement for South American papers," March 9, 1921.

Washington, D.C., Secretary of Commerce Hoover laid down the principle that "no nation should itself or should permit its citizens to borrow money from foreign countries, and no nation should allow its citizens to loan money to foreign countries unless this money is to be devoted to productive enterprise."[13] In this oblique commentary on "dollar diplomacy," he went on to say that money loaned for military equipment or war purposes was a threat to peace. Hoover's remarks brought the quick reaction from the Department of State that his principle "was not in accord with its policy" on the American continent.[14]

As a result of his early interests in the nations to the south and his contacts with them, during his eight years with the Department of Commerce, Hoover acquired a comprehensive grasp of the possibilities of expanding trade between Latin America and the United States. Upon the growing importance of this expansion he dwelt again and again in his annual reports.

When Calvin Coolidge was inaugurated President in his "own right" on March 4, 1925, he started with a new Secretary of State, Frank B. Kellogg. Sumner Welles, a later New Deal Democrat, labeled the period after Hughes' departure from the Department of State the "unhappy four years," in which inter-American relations deteriorated.[15] While Secretary of State Kellogg labored with Foreign Minister Aristide Briand of France to outlaw war in the world, American bayonets were upholding peace and security in Nicaragua and Haiti.

For a short while in 1925 the occupying force of United States Marines was withdrawn from Nicaragua. But within a month, the embers of revolution again burst into flame. This caused the Coolidge administration to look upon the withdrawal as premature, and the Marines were sent back the following year. Complications had set in when Coolidge recognized one warring faction in Nicaragua as legal and Mexico recognized another. As a consequence of the rivalry, the United States placed an embargo on arms going to the Liberal faction, headed by Dr. Juan B. Sacasa, but allowed arms to flow freely to the regime of Adolfo Díaz, who paid for them with money advanced in American loans.[16]

[13] *New York Times*, May 3, 1927.
[14] *Ibid.*
[15] Sumner Welles, *The Time for Decision*, p. 188.
[16] For a detailed account of the events of this period, see Department of State, *The United States and Nicaragua*, pp. 55–68.

Because of its "private war" in Nicaragua, the Coolidge adminis-tration ran into a buzz saw of criticism, both at home and in Latin America.[17] In defense of its actions, the administration raised the specter of Communist activity in the republics to the south, besides citing evidence that Mexico was actively aiding the Sacasa forces by supplying them with arms.[18] But the alarm of Comintern machina-tions failed to arouse the hoped-for public support. An enterprising newspaper correspondent succeeded in reaching Sacasa's headquar-ters and saw no evidence of Mexican intervention. In fact, he found Sacasa a man who was disposed to be friendly toward the United States, despite the antagonism of the Coolidge administration.[19]

Sensitive to criticism, Coolidge defended his policies. Stung into action, in March 1927 he dispatched Henry L. Stimson, former Sec-retary of War, to Nicaragua as his personal representative. Stimson had full power to mediate a settlement between the factions in the re-public. After a series of exasperating negotiations, Stimson was able to bring both factions to an agreement, thereby also improving rela-tions with the United States.[20] One of the rebel chieftains, however, refused to be pacified. He was Augusto César Sandino, who was to haunt United States-Nicaraguan relations again.

Relations with Mexico also became strained in this period, pri-marily over the enforcement of the Mexican alien-land and petroleum laws of December 1925,[21] as well as over the Nicaraguan imbroglio. The president of Mexico, Plutarco Elias Calles, believed the provi-

[17] The Nicaragua affair was also subject to a bitter attack in Congress. See *Con-gressional Record,* 69th Cong., 2d sess., pp. 1427–29. Kellogg's biographer states: "Nothing during the postwar period proved more conducive to distrust of the United States, whether justified or not, than the events which occurred in Nicaragua." David Bryn-Jones, *Frank B. Kellogg,* p. 196.

[18] See Coolidge's message of January 10, 1927, *Congressional Record,* 69th Cong., 2d sess., pp. 1324–26. He said he had "conclusive evidence" of arms being shipped to the rebels from Mexico.

[19] William Philip Simms, foreign editor of the Scripps-Howard Newspaper Al-liance, personal interview, Washington, D.C., June 26, 1948. Mr. Simms was the first American correspondent to reach the Sacasa forces. See his interview with Sacasa in the *San Diego Sun,* January 14, 1927; also his dispatches of January 15, 18, and 24, 1927.

[20] For Stimson's personal account of the settlement, see Henry L. Stimson, *American Policy in Nicaragua,* chap. ii.

[21] These laws were designed to put into operation theretofore unfulfilled pro-visions of the constitution of 1917, relating to the acquisition of agricultural land in Mexico by foreigners and the reversion to national ownership of the subsoil deposits of Mexican land. For an extended discussion, see James M. Callahan, *American Foreign Policy in Mexican Relations,* pp. 597 ff.

sions of the land and petroleum laws to be retroactive. If so interpreted, these provisions would have deprived American capitalists in Mexico of the subsoil rights of the property they owned. This was of utmost concern to American investors, as the primary reason for investing in Mexico was the lucrative subsoil mineral wealth of the land. The Coolidge administration chose to heed the wails of American business in Mexico, and relations with that country were in volcanic condition until the appointment of Dwight W. Morrow, a Wall Street lawyer and financier, as ambassador to Mexico in September 1927. Morrow promptly applied himself to a thorough study of his task, and with tact and diplomacy helped bring about a gradual improvement in relations.[22]

A timely decision, favorable to American petroleum interests, by the Mexican Supreme Court on November 17, 1927, pacified American capital. The ambassador's task was also aided by Colonel Charles A. Lindbergh's nonstop flight from Washington, D.C., to Mexico City, on December 14, 1929. Lindbergh was then the toast of the continent. His flight was made at the behest of Morrow and was unique in its effect upon Mexican public opinion and upon diplomatic relations with Mexico. The airplane and the hero became the tools of the diplomat.

A factor that was accountable for much of Morrow's success was that he liked the Mexicans and they liked him.[23] A former president of Mexico, Emilio Portes Gil, expressed admiration for the ambassador when he characterized him as a man with a great heart, great finesse, and distinction; a humane diplomat who studied Mexican ways and needs.[24]

The question of American imperialism was hotly debated at the Rio de Janeiro meeting of the International Commission of American Jurists, which was in session from April 18 to May 20, 1927.[25] United States intervention was severely castigated, and the Nicaraguan representative in Mexico sent a telegram to the gathering asking it to make an express declaration condemning the policy of the United States in Latin America.[26] This gave rise to a heated political debate,

[22] Stuart, *op. cit.,* pp. 180–82. Gives a clear picture of Morrow's diplomacy.
[23] See Harold Nicolson, *Dwight Morrow,* p. 299.
[24] Emilio Portes Gil, *Quince años de política mexicana,* p. 356.
[25] For an authoritative account of this meeting, see James B. Scott, "The Gradual and Progressive Codification of International Law," *Bulletin of the Pan American Union,* LXI (September 1927), 849–70.
[26] Dexter Perkins, *Hands Off: A History of the Monroe Doctrine,* pp. 339–40.

but the real conflict came about when the conference adopted, by acclamation, a formula which declared that "no state could interfere in the internal affairs of another."[27] After vainly trying to suppress the obnoxious resolution, the United States representatives, who were anxious to avoid any clash at Rio that might prejudice the prospects of the forthcoming conference of American states at Havana, acquiesced in its adoption.[28]

An inauspicious stage had thus been set for the Sixth International Conference of American States that met in Havana, Cuba, from January 16 to February 20, 1928.[29] Owing to the formidable increase in the financial and economic power of the United States in comparison to her sister republics, the current of opposition to the "northern giant" had been steadily mounting for years, and the situation was nearing a climax. To make things worse, American intervention in Nicaragua was an undeniable fact, upon which the wrath of the southern nations focused. The tide of Pan-Americanism was at its lowest ebb, and a concerted attack on the United States was expected. To forestall this and to emphasize the seriousness of the situation, President Coolidge broke precedent and attended the conference personally. As an added measure, he appointed an exceptionally strong delegation, headed by Charles E. Hughes, to represent the United States.[30] But it was only after persistent urging by Secretary of State Kellogg, and the stressing of the crucial character of the occasion, that Coolidge accepted the invitation advanced by President Machado of Cuba to make the opening speech of the conference.[31] This was the first time during his presidency that Coolidge set foot on foreign soil, and the second time that an American President visited a Latin-American country.[32]

As was to be expected, the attack on United States intervention came after lengthy discussion. It was spearheaded by Dr. Gustavo

[27] Dexter Perkins, *Hands Off: A History of the Monroe Doctrine*, pp. 339–40.

[28] See Arnold J. Toynbee, *Survey of International Affairs, 1927*, pp. 425–26. Hereafter cited as Toynbee, *International Affairs*.

[29] For documents and proceedings, see James B. Scott, ed., *The International Conferences of American States, 1889–1928*, pp. 295 ff.

[30] "The Sixth Pan-American Conference," Part I, *Foreign Policy Association Information Service*, IV (April 1928), 50. This is an excellent account of the proceedings of the conference.

[31] See Bryn-Jones, *op. cit.*, p. 197. Apparently Kellogg was more aware of the need for fence-mending than was the President.

[32] Only two other Presidents had previously left American soil while in office: Woodrow Wilson went to Europe and Theodore Roosevelt visited Panama.

Guerrero of El Salvador and by the Mexican and Argentine delegates. Dr. Guerrero at the plenary session of February 20 presented a motion to the conference that "no state has the right to intervene in the internal affairs of another." This was in line with the 1927 Rio formula. The leader of the United States delegation, former Secretary of State Hughes, arose in a vigorous reply and proclaimed that "We want no aggression" and "do not wish the territory of any American Republic. We do not wish to govern any American Republic" nor "to intervene in the affairs of any American Republic."[33] But at the same time he openly defended the past "interpositions" in Latin America by the United States, making this the last public defense of American intervention policies. Dr. Guerrero withdrew his motion.

The Argentine delegation attacked the tariff policy of the United States and made several proposals to remedy trade difficulties, quoting Herbert Hoover to support its position.[34] Hughes successfully opposed the Argentine proposals. This diplomatic defeat galled the Argentine delegation and led its chairman, Honorio Pueyrredón, to resign both from this post and as ambassador to the United States.[35] Although Hughes' statesmanship averted an open break, anti-American sentiment continued to smolder in many of the Latin-American states, and the effects were to be felt later by the Hoover administration. The last inter-American event of major importance that occurred during the Coolidge administration was the meeting in Washington, D.C., from December 10, 1928, to January 5, 1929, of the International Conference of American States on Conciliation and Arbitration. The gathering was held pursuant to a resolution adopted at the Havana Conference.[36] As a result of extended deliberations, three important instruments were signed: a general treaty of arbitration, a protocol of progressive arbitration, and a general convention of international conciliation.[37] All the member countries of the Pan American Union, except Argentina, attended the conference.

During the administrations of Harding and Coolidge, Hoover

[33] "The Sixth Pan-American Conference," op. cit., pp. 71–72.

[34] See ibid., pp. 57–60.

[35] Toynbee, op. cit., p. 437.

[36] "International Conference of American States on Conciliation and Arbitration," Bulletin of the Pan American Union, LXIII (February 1929), 113.

[37] See ibid., pp. 114–27, for texts. These conciliation and arbitration agreements, together with the Gondra Treaty of 1923, were vital parts of the peace machinery of the American nations.

had held the chairmanship of the Inter-American High Commission. This position, along with his cabinet post of Secretary of Commerce, gave him a knowledge of Latin America, its peoples, and its problems. His contacts with Latin America during eight years as a cabinet officer aroused his interest in the southern continent and gave him an appreciation of the possibilities of trade and of political and cultural exchange with the southern half of the Western Hemisphere.

During the administrations of the twentieth century, from Theodore Roosevelt to Calvin Coolidge, the Latin-American relations of the United States had deteriorated badly, owing primarily to a series of interventions by the United States in the Caribbean area.

In the closing days of his presidential term, Coolidge suddenly realized, through pressure of public opinion, the deplorable state of inter-American relations. In hasty, last-minute efforts he tried to improve them. This changed attitude toward Latin-American affairs had its beginnings less than a year before Hoover was elected President of the United States. With the stage thus set, it was not coincidental or strange that one of Herbert Hoover's first acts, after his election to the presidency, was to turn southward.

CHAPTER II

THE GOOD-WILL TOUR

"I made a journey through South America prior to inauguration for the purpose of dissipating the fears and antagonisms which had grown up amongst these states as to the intentions and policies of our Government." —HERBERT C. HOOVER, 1933

When on November 6, 1928, Herbert Clark Hoover was elected thirty-first President of the United States, he rode high on a wave of postwar prosperity that swept him into the White House with the greatest vote that any man had yet received from the American people.[1] Hoover's election seemed to presage four years of exceptional government. In the domestic affairs of the nation all was going well. The American public was basking in the sunlight of plenty, and American capital was pushing ahead into new and untried frontiers. The former Secretary of Commerce, with eight years' experience in prosperous American government, intended to maintain this exhilarating tempo of life.

In the field of international affairs, Hoover was different from the conventional successful politician. He was no strait-laced provincial; he was a man of breadth, of international prominence.[2] His profession and his direction of relief work had taken him all over the world; as Secretary of Commerce his administrative ability had raised the Department of Commerce to a new level of importance. The name Hoover was known throughout the world. According to some observers, "it was said with truth that no President of the United States, unless it were John Quincy Adams, had come to the office so fully

---

[1] Edgar E. Robinson, *The Presidential Vote, 1896–1932,* p. 24. Contains an excellent analysis of the presidential election. Hoover received 58.12 percent of the vote cast and Alfred E. Smith, his Democratic opponent, received 40.80 percent.

[2] In an editorial, *La Prensa* (Buenos Aires), November 8, 1928, hailed the election and remarked that it was not as much a triumph of Republicans over Democrats as a victory of Hoover's personality over Smith's. It characterized Coolidge as "provincial"; one whose horizon was limited to internal affairs even when viewing the world. By contrast, it called Hoover a man with a broad international background.

equipped with a comprehensive knowledge of the foreign relations of America."[3]

In his speech accepting the Republican nomination for President, Hoover sounded the keynote of his administration's foreign policy by declaring that "our foreign policy has one primary object, and that is peace. We have no hates; we wish no further possessions; we harbor no military threats."[4] This attitude was well in keeping with his Quaker background and with his experience as an engineer, which led him to hate the waste of war.

A few weeks after his election, President-elect Hoover started on a good-will tour of Latin America, the only part of the world he had not at some time visited.[5] When Hoover announced his intention of embarking on this preinauguration trip, speculation ran rampant in the press of the Western Hemisphere as to his reasons for taking such a journey.[6] The Latin Americans were generally pleased and somewhat flattered by the attention suddenly focused on them.[7] In deciding to make such a long voyage Hoover was apparently motivated by a desire to implement the ideal of the "good neighbor," by getting to know his southern neighbors and by trying to dissipate their fears concerning the intentions and policies of the United States. "Our trip to Latin America," he said simply, "was conceived for the purpose of paying friendly calls upon our neighbors to the south."[8]

[3] From an editorial in the *New York Times,* September 8, 1929. For a violent anti-American attack on Hoover, see Alfredo L. Palacios, *Nuestra América y el imperialismo yanqui,* pp. 108–10.

[4] Delivered August 11, 1929, at Palo Alto, California. See *The New Day: Campaign Speeches of Herbert Hoover, 1928,* p. 38.

[5] John Barrett, former director general of the Pan American Union, had suggested similar trips to Wilson and Harding after their elections. See *New York Evening Post,* November 17, 1928, and *New York Times,* November 10, 1928. No American President or President-elect had ever before taken so long a journey to other countries.

[6] *O Paiz* (Rio de Janeiro), December 21, 1928. An article by Daniel de Carvalho made the point that the trip was taken to counteract certain effects produced during the election compaign in which most sections of Latin America favored Smith. Hoover was pictured as a Republican imperialist of the Taft-Coolidge tradition, whereas Smith was favored as a pacifist, a Democrat, and a Catholic. See also editorial in *La Prensa* (Buenos Aires), November 6, 1928.

[7] See editorial in *La Prensa* (Buenos Aires), November 11, 1928.

[8] Harry W. Hill, ed., *President-elect Herbert Hoover's Good-Will Cruise to Central and South America,* p. 9. By taking this trip, Hoover skillfully avoided possible differences with Coolidge during the awkward interregnum from election to inauguration.

Basically, Hoover saw the trip as a means of taking the first step in what was to be a reorientation of policy toward Latin America.[9]

In a statement to the press, shortly before departing for the southern continent, Hoover declared, "I have had the suggestion of a visit to certain Latin-American countries before me for several days. It has been cordially supported by President Coolidge and Secretary Kellogg."[10] With official sanction granted, the President-elect's trip was liable to have an important bearing on the direction of the nation's Latin-American policy.[11]

Even before he left his own home, Hoover was made rudely aware of the strong feeling that United States intervention had aroused in the banana republics. A few minutes before his special train left Palo Alto, California, for San Pedro, where he was to sail for Central American waters, a small group carrying banners caused a commotion, denouncing American imperialism and intervention in Nicaragua.[12] Actually, few persons in the gay farewell crowd knew of the disturbance, as it was quickly dissipated. Neither Mr. nor Mrs. Hoover saw the demonstration, but the President-elect "was considerably troubled over the incident."[13] This episode was perhaps symptomatic of the need for a change in inter-American relations.

Henry P. Fletcher accompanied Hoover as official adviser, and also acted as personal representative of President Coolidge and of the Department of State. Ambassador Fletcher had had long diplomatic service in Latin-American countries, and possessed an intimate knowledge of their affairs. Thus, proper precaution was taken to assure cordial and intelligent intercourse between Latin-American officials and the President-elect's party. Along with the official party went numerous American newspapermen and photographers—the great-

[9] Interview with William P. Simms, June 26, 1948. Mr. Simms was with Mr. Hoover on the tour, and often discussed aspects of Latin-American policy with him. See Simms's articles in the *San Diego Sun,* November 19 and 30, 1928.

[10] Quoted in the *New York Times,* November 10, 1928.

[11] Gaston Nerval, a Bolivian and a severe critic of American foreign policy, praised the contemplated voyage. He declared the visit "will accomplish more . . . . than all the labors of the numerous diplomatic missions put together." See *Washington Star,* November 18, 1928; also Edmundo Gutiérrez, "Hoover-Yrigoyen-Leguía," *Aconcagua,* II (December 1928), 11–14.

[12] See the *Palo Alto Times,* November 19, 1928; also the *New York Times,* November 19, 1928.

[13] Rex Collier in the *Washington Star,* January 21, 1929. In a series of articles in the January and February 1929 issues of the *Star,* Collier gave one of the best accounts of the trip. He knew Hoover personally, and accompanied him throughout the tour.

est invasion of foreign newspapermen ever recorded in the history of the South American continent up to that time.[14] Some sections of the Latin-American press registered disappointment over a ruling which made it impossible for Latin-American newspaper correspondents to be included in the press contingent.[15] To ensure smooth relations and to stress the importance of the trip, President Coolidge let it be known that Hoover was to be accorded presidential honors even though he had not yet been inaugurated as chief executive.

The President-elect and his party started their cruise from San Pedro, California, on November 19, 1928, aboard the battleship U.S.S. *Maryland*. The ten-week tour took them to Honduras, El Salvador, Nicaragua, Costa Rica, Ecuador, Peru, Chile, Argentina, Uruguay, and Brazil. Hoover delivered some twenty-five addresses en route. While the trip was in progress, public reaction to the undertaking in the United States was generally favorable, as was editorial comment, though there was criticism from some quarters. The *Saturday Evening Post* envisaged a new era in inter-American relations growing from the journey. "No happier choice," it commented, "of an ambassador of good will could have been made."[16] A prominent Chilean newspaper agreed that "it will be the first time the White House has been occupied by a man knowing Latin America."[17] A Brazilian columnist exulted that "Hoover . . . . represents the modern principle of co-operation and solidarity."[18] Throughout *América del Sur* editorial comment on Hoover and his visit was on the whole favorable; as *La Prensa* of Buenos Aires succinctly phrased it, "Hoover comes at a good time."[19]

But there were a few discordant notes in the symphony of praise. One critic described the trip as a "trade junket in the interests of big business." Others questioned the use of a battleship in making the trip and the expense involved.[20] Many European papers were skep-

---

[14] *Buenos Aires Herald,* December 12, 1928.

[15] Rex Collier, *Washington Star,* January 22, 1929, and *Literary Digest,* December 8, 1928, p. 15. The exigencies of time and space apparently made this ruling necessary.

[16] "Our Ambassador of Good Will," editorial in the *Saturday Evening Post,* December 15, 1928, p. 24.

[17] Quoted in *Literary Digest,* November 24, 1928, p. 7.

[18] Daniel de Carvalho in *O Paiz* (Rio de Janeiro), December 21, 1928.

[19] Cf. editorial columns in *La Nación* (Santiago, Chile), December 11, 1928; *La Nación* (Buenos Aires), December 13, 1928; *La Prensa* (Buenos Aires), November 30, 1928; and *La Nueva Prensa* (San José, Costa Rica), November 28, 1928.

[20] Hoover paid for the expenses of the trip out of his own pocket, except for the press representatives, who paid their own way. It was alleged that since both

tical or looked with alarm at the possible loss of Europe's Latin-American trade to the United States.[21] Hispanic-American critics were not entirely dormant. Sections of the Argentine and Uruguayan press scored American intervention in the Caribbean and evinced disappointment over the knowledge that Hoover could spend only one day in each of the capitals visited.[22] *El Diario* of Montevideo, Uruguay, was hostile to the trip, chiefly on the ground that "Mr. Hoover, as heir to the Latin-American policy of the Republican administration, represented a spirit absolutely contrary to the nationalistic sentiment of Hispanic America."[23] From the United States there came charges of press censorship imposed on the correspondents who accompanied Hoover on the trip.[24] These allegations were probably prompted by the supervision "necessitated by Navy regulations governing the use of ships' radio."[25] Censorship of press copy was harmless on both the *Maryland* and the *Utah* (which carried the President-elect home). In addition, reporters were free to send any kind of copy while ashore, "and on landing at Hampton Roads the correspondents found themselves almost, if not actually, defending the system."[26]

Many of Hoover's speeches and statements in Latin America were friendly expressions of good will and simple neighborliness that did not touch upon the vital political questions of the day; for, at the time, he was not an official member of the United States government. But several of his statements went beyond the neighborly utterances of amity and were indicative of future policy, to be followed when he took over the reins of government. In his first address to a Hispanic-American audience, delivered at Amapala, Honduras, on November 26, 1928, the President-elect foretold the new policy of the United States toward Latin America. He expressed a new concern over inter-American relations. Embracing the ideal of the "good neighbor" in

the U.S.S. *Maryland* and the U.S.S. *Utah* were under steam at all times, no added expense was incurred in their use. See Hoover Papers, George Akerson, Hoover's personal secretary, to Edwin Freeland of Tulsa, Okla., May 15, 1929.

[21] See *La Prensa* (Buenos Aires), November 14, 1928; also Edwin Emerson, *Hoover and His Times,* pp. 72–73.

[22] See *El País* (Montevideo), December 17, 1928; also editorial in *La Prensa* (Buenos Aires), November 23, 1928.

[23] Quoted in N. A. N. Cleven, "President-Elect Hoover's Visit to South America," *Current History,* XXIX (January 1929), 683.

[24] See *Congressional Record,* 70th Cong., 2d sess., pp. 2051–52.

[25] See Rex Collier in the *Washington Star,* January 22, 1929.

[26] *Ibid.*

international relations, he applied it specifically to inter-American relations and defined some of the responsibilities of a "good neighbor." In part he declared:

> I come to pay a call of friendship. In a sense I represent on this occasion the people of the United States extending a friendly greeting to our fellow democracies on the American continent. I would wish to symbolize the friendly visit of one *good neighbor* to another. In our daily life, *good neighbors* call upon each other as the evidence of solicitude for the common welfare and to learn of the circumstances and point of view of each, so that there may come both understanding and respect which are the cementing forces of all enduring society. This should be equally true amongst nations. We have a desire to maintain not only the cordial relations of governments with each other but the relations of *good neighbors*.[27]

At Hoover's third port of call, Corinto, Nicaragua, the tour met a crucial test. All of Latin America's anti–United States sentiment was focused in this republic and was brought to a boiling point by the occupation. Here the President-elect gave evidence of statesmanship by bringing together in one meeting three of Nicaragua's leading political figures who had until lately been in deadly conflict.[28] Here also, while barely started, the tour was almost wrecked.

Some of the more radical elements in the Liberal party had hatched a plot which they hoped would disorganize the tour and express a protest against American intervention. It was due chiefly to William P. Simms, who was one of the accredited correspondents in the touring party, that the plot never came to life. Through a series of "cloak and dagger" episodes, Simms learned that a number of well-planned demonstrations and riots were slated to take place before Hoover and his party left Nicaragua. Many of the plotters were members of the Sacasa faction whom Simms had known in 1927.

Because of the favorable news reports Simms wrote about their cause at that time, he was still a *persona grata* to the Sacasa group. Simms worked hard to dissuade the schemers. He told them that

---

[27] *Addresses Delivered During the Visit of Herbert Hoover, President-elect of the United States, to Central and South America, November–December 1928,* p. 3. (Italics inserted.) Hereafter cited as *Hoover's Latin-American Addresses.* Cf. Franklin D. Roosevelt's use of the term "good neighbor" in his inaugural address, *Congressional Record,* 73d Cong., special session, p. 5, and in his first Pan American Day address, Department of State Press Releases, No. 185 (April 15, 1933), p. 244.

[28] They were former President Emiliano Chamorro, President Adolfo Díaz, and President-Elect José María Moncada. See *New York Times,* November 28, 1928, and Hoover, *Latin-American Addresses,* p. 9.

they would make a great mistake if they tried to carry out their plot; that they would be doing their cause and their country incalculable harm. Simms also impressed upon them that Hoover was their friend, that he was no interventionist, and that he was taking this trip to learn to know and understand them and their people.[29] Apparently Simms was successful in his appeal, for the reception in Nicaragua went on without embarrassing occurrences.

Both Simms and Hoover attached great importance to this affair. The conspirators, if successful, could have wrecked the entire trip. Demonstrations of the kind contemplated might have served as the first link in a chain reaction throughout Latin America, and set the pattern to be followed by all the radical groups in the countries to be visited. As it was, no unpleasant precedent was established.

At Lima, Peru, Hoover was given a splendid welcome.[30] He responded by indicating that inter-American relations would be of primary importance in his administration and would warrant his personal attention and investigation. As he assured his audience,

. . . . I have come for other purposes than recreation or to receive personal satisfactions of travel. I have had the hope and the aspiration that I could serve in some way to further reinforce the structure of peace and friendship, the unity of ideals which have remained unbroken since the birth of our republics. I have thought that I could better prepare myself for the task by a widened knowledge of the men and problems of our sister republics.[31]

After this address, and his short visit in Peru, the Quaker statesman and his party went on to Chile, arriving at Antofagasta on December 8, 1928. From there, the party went to Santiago, Chile, where Hoover was formally greeted by President Carlos Ibáñez. The reception given America's good-will ambassador was at first cool and courteous. This was attributed to the intense feeling over the Tacna-Arica dispute,[32] and to Hoover's previous talks with President Augusto B. Leguía of Peru, Alberto Palacios, minister of foreign affairs of Bolivia, and other officials of these countries, who, together with the Chileans, were vitally interested in the settlement of the enigmatic "question of the Pacific." At Santiago Hoover again reiterated

[29] Personal interview with William P. Simms, June 26, 1948.
[30] For tributes and public acclaim accorded Hoover, see *El excelentísimo señor Herbert Clark Hoover presidente electo de los Estados Unidos de América visita el Perú 5 de diciembre de 1928.*
[31] *Hoover's Latin-American Addresses,* pp. 21–22.
[32] The settlement of this problem is discussed at length in chapter iii.

the principle he had put forth as Secretary of Commerce—that foreign loans for the development of public works and commerce were beneficial to both borrower and lender. In Chile, he left less anti-American sentiment than he found there, and sowed the seeds of sincere friendship.[33]

The good-will tour then crossed the towering Andes into Argentina, and the U.S.S. *Maryland* returned to the United States. Prior to the crossing of the mountain barrier, Argentine police had allegedly discovered a bomb plot to blow up the President-elect's special train. The importance of the affair proved to be greatly exaggerated, and scant attention was paid to it by either Hoover or members of his party.[34]

In crossing the vast Argentine pampas, Hoover was a little disappointed by the coldness of his reception at the small whistle stops along the way. Instead of the usual friendly, gay, and colorful crowds with which he had become familiar in the first part of the trip, he found no friendly demonstrations or greetings; only apathetic, apparently uninformed and listless groups of peasants.[35] Of course, in most instances, the warmth of the receptions was set by the attitude of the particular government, and here government initiative was evidently lacking. Because of the purported conspiracy, the Argentine government instituted drastic military precautions to safeguard the distinguished visitor's train as it approached the capital; "every foot of the route into the city" had been placed under elaborate military and police guard.[36] While designed to allay alarm on the part of the Hoover mission, these grim preparations had the opposite effect. They gave evidence of political unrest, and the government's fear of a possible uprising.

At Buenos Aires it was necessary for Hoover to impress most strongly the idea that the United States intended to adopt the ideal of the "good neighbor" and to follow a course of good will toward Latin America. Argentina was the center of resistance to "Yankee

---

[33] Hoover Papers, letter from Warren C. Grahame to Hoover's personal secretary, Lawrence Richey, March 25, 1929, containing a confidential report on the effects of the tour, by C. H. Abbot; also a letter from the American ambassador to Chile, W. S. Culbertson, to President Hoover, May 13, 1929.

[34] *Buenos Aires Herald,* December 12, 1928. An investigating *Herald* reporter found some truth in the news about the conspiracy, but also found that most of the excitement was caused by exaggerated rumors.

[35] Simms interview, June 26, 1948.

[36] *Buenos Aires Herald,* December 12, 1928, and Rex Collier in the *Washington Star,* February 18, 1929.

imperialism," and it considered itself the leader and champion of Latin-American civilization. Even before Hoover started his trip, there had been difficulty with the proud-spirited empire of wheat and cattle. When the good-will tour was planned, Dr. Hipólito Irigoyen, president of the Argentine Republic, delayed the courtesy of extending the future President of the United States an invitation to visit Argentina so long that Dr. Manuel E. Malbrán, the Argentine ambassador in Washington, made a hurried visit to his homeland to protest Irigoyen's slowness.[37] After President Coolidge made it known that Hoover was to be accorded presidential honors, Irigoyen sent him a belated invitation.

On its arrival in Buenos Aires, the good-neighbor mission found evidences of anti–United States demonstrations, undoubtedly stemming from resentment over America's policy in Nicaragua. Hoover soon helped clear the atmosphere by the judicious use of a phrase that pleased the Argentine ego. He referred to Argentina as the "world's bread basket." The slogan *"la canasta de pan del mundo"* was quickly taken up by the Argentine press, and was soon known throughout the land, along with its author. *El Diario* of Buenos Aires ran headlines of the phrase in all editions and commented that "we are glad that such an expression came from Mr. Hoover, who is a highly qualified judge."[38]

It was also in Buenos Aires that the Quaker statesman made what was perhaps his most significant pronouncement on future policy. In an exclusive interview granted the Buenos Aires newspaper, *La Nación*, Hoover denounced the "big brother" concept of relations between the United States and the other countries of the Western Hemisphere, and he also renounced the principle of United States intervention. He thus foreshadowed a repudiation of Theodore Roosevelt's corollary to the Monroe Doctrine, by declaring:

The idea has persisted for a long time that among nations, as in families, there are younger and older brothers. One deduces from this idea that the function of acting as a tutor, at least in spiritual matters and many times in matters of policing, is exercised by the older brothers with the supposed younger brothers.

I absolutely disapprove such sentimental or political doctrines or views. There are no young independent sovereign nations, there are no older and

---

[37] Walter Lippmann and William O. Scroggs, eds., *The United States in World Affairs, 1931,* p. 65.

[38] Quoted in the *New York Times,* December 15, 1928. See also *Argentina.* II (January 1929), 5–6.

younger brothers on the American continent. All are of the same age from a
political and spiritual viewpoint . . . .

I see in each nation of the continent a friendly nation and each the same
age, friendly and equal States of a great continent in which great nations progress along an even line as a group of friends as friendly or more so than
brothers with similar ideals, which lead in new directions to new purposes, all
close together and all at equal levels.

The fear of some persons concerning supposed intervention ideas of the
United States are unfounded. The facts are gradually demonstrating more
clearly and more fully that in my country there prevails no policy of intervention, despite any appearances of such an intention.[39]

This interview aroused some criticism in the United States as to
the basis of Hoover's authority for commenting on government policy
when he was still a private citizen. But in Argentina, Hoover's reported utterances on intervention were favorably received.[40]

La Época, another Argentine newspaper, published an interview
granted by President Irigoyen, in which he said that Hoover had
promised him "that the United States under his coming administration would abstain from further intervention in the internal affairs
of Latin America."[41] Some Latin skeptics expressed hope that
Hoover's administration might "prove the declaration more than
wind blowing across the Pampas." All in all, Hoover's brief sojourn
in Argentine was surprisingly successful. His visit and his private
talks with Argentine officials helped considerably to dispel the fear
and distrust of the United States that had been evident before his
coming. Indications of the influence Hoover wielded were shown by
the change of attitude on the part of some of the Argentine press.
After his brief stay, several important Argentine newspapers urged
closer relation with Tío Sam.[42]

Uruguay's attitude toward the North American good-will mission was similar to that of Argentina.[43] An effort to stage an anti-
intervention demonstration upon Hoover's arrival was squelched by
the Uruguayan security forces. But the agitators caused enough concern to prompt the authorities to abandon the originally planned

[39] New York Times, December 17, 1928.
[40] Hoover Papers, C. H. Abbot in the Grahame letter of March 25, 1929.
[41] Quoted in Emerson, op. cit., pp. 43–44.
[42] Hoover Papers, letter from Leo S. Rowe, director general of the Pan American Union, to President Hoover, December 10, 1929. Rowe stressed La Prensa's
change of tone. It had earlier been critical of Hoover. See favorable editorial in
La Prensa (Buenos Aires), December 24, 1928.
[43] Hoover Papers, C. H. Abbot in the Grahame letter of March 25, 1929.

parade through the city of Montevideo.[44] The President-elect made a forceful speech in Montevideo. He lashed out at the causes of misunderstanding among nations, and stressed the need for respect, friendship, and mutual helpfulness between them. He compared relations between nations to "the relations between *neighbors*," and explained that "I have hoped that I might by this visit symbolize the courtesy of a call from one *good neighbor* to another, that I might convey the respect, esteem and desire for intellectual and spiritual co-operation."[45]

From Uruguay, the Spanish-speaking buffer state, the Hoover party crossed into Portuguese-speaking Brazil. It arrived in Rio de Janeiro on December 21, 1928, where Hoover received the greatest ovation of his tour. He was given "a welcome such as few men ever received in Brazil . . . . or in any other South American nation."[46] He was greeted with an amazing spectacle of splendor; a gay holiday spirit prevailed throughout the city, and vast, happy throngs symbolized Brazilian and American friendship by waving star-spangled flags and the green, yellow, and blue colors of Brazil. Hoover responded warmly to the gala reception by expressing gratitude for the "overwhelming" honor paid him and his country. He strongly stressed the long, unbroken record of mutual good will "which has become a precious tradition between us."[47]

At Rio, Hoover and his entourage boarded the battleship U.S.S. *Utah,* which was waiting in the harbor. The tour thus ended on a high note of good will and cordiality.

No one individual and no one voyage, such as the good-will trip, could completely put at rest past fears and suspicions of the United States in Latin America, or bring about a transformation in inter-American relations. The most that could be expected was a successful launching of a new program based upon mutual understanding. Hoover launched such a program. When he sailed for the United States, distrust and old fears had already begun to fade. Also, it was noteworthy that even before he stepped into the White House, Hoover chose to shore up a sagging section of the nation's foreign policy. The good-will tour was pregnant with meaning for the future in that the new chief executive made it patent to all that Latin-American relations

[44] Rex Collier in the *Washington Star,* February 21, 1929.
[45] *Hoover's Latin-American Addresses,* p. 36. Italics inserted.
[46] *New York Times,* December 22, 1928.
[47] See *Hoover's Latin-American Addresses,* p. 48.

had become a most important question of foreign policy. His trip fixed the attention of his own people upon important and growing nations of which they were placidly ignorant.[48] It also focused the eyes of the United States upon foreign affairs in a period of growing isolationism. From his friendly visit Hoover gathered first-hand information on trade conditions in the southern continent, and he gained an opportunity to sense the political and national spirit of the long-neglected Latin neighbors. Thus, he was able to build, from his first-hand knowledge, the foundation for an improved Latin-American policy, based upon his own concept of the "good neighbor" in intra-hemispheric relations.[49]

Except for a few incidents, the tour was a success. As a rule, the future American President was received with acclaim and was feted warmly, although receptions ranged from cool and formal in Argentina to joyously frenzied in Brazil.[50] His words awakened lively sympathy throughout Latin America, because he showed discerning knowledge of the problems and peoples of the southern continent. His presence in the southern republics centered attention on that particular part of the world in the press, in the magazines, on the radio, and in popular conversation in the United States. Publicity and information became the highway for better understanding.

Few were the instances in the past when relations between the Americas were as friendly as at the conclusion of the good-will journey. Undoubtedly, the opportunity given to Latin Americans to meet and see the future head of the "colossus of the north" brought about hopes on their part for a new spirit of equality, friendliness, and what they conceived to be justice on the part of the incoming administration.[51] Early in the tour Hoover had remarked that "good will between nations is not a policy—it is a deduction arising from a series of actions. It is not a diplomatic formula; it is an aspiration which flows from the ideals of a people."[52] Certainly, the tour was the first strong pillar in building good will through a series of actions.

[48] See William P. Simms in the *San Diego Sun*, January 7, 1929; also Frank H. Simonds, "Hoover, South Americanus," *Review of Reviews*, LXXIX (February 1929), 68.

[49] Personal interview with Herbert C. Hoover at Stanford University, Stanford, California, August 5, 1947. Cf. statement in *New York Times*, December 13, 1943; William P. Simms in *Washington Daily News*, June 24, 1948; and Eugene Lyons, *Our Unknown Ex-President*, p. 243.

[50] See François de Tessan, *Le président Hoover et la politique américaine*, p. 119.

[51] See *La Prensa* (Buenos Aires), December 24, 1928.

[52] *Hoover's Latin-American Addresses*, p. 12.

CHAPTER III

LENDING A HELPING HAND

"The co-operation which the United States has lent to this work of American harmony that has just ended in a solemn ceremony commands the gratitude of Chile, and I therefore fulfill the high duty of so expressing it to the Arbiter whose weighty and delicate work ends in the international act concluded on this day."

—PRESIDENT IBÁÑEZ OF CHILE TO PRESIDENT HOOVER,
June 3, 1929

While Hoover was on his good-will tour of Latin America, he made it a point to sound out the views of the interested governments on the possibility of reaching a final settlement of the fifty-year-old Tacna-Arica dispute. This "question of the Pacific" was a festering sore that had defied settlement since the signing of the Treaty of Ancón[1] between Chile and Peru at the close of the bloody and costly War of the Pacific of 1879–1883, in which Chile had decisively defeated Peru and Bolivia.[2] Through the treaty, Chile gained, among other things, possession of the frontier provinces of Tacna and Arica for a period of ten years, with a stipulation that upon the expiration of this term a plebiscite should be held to determine their ultimate ownership. The country that retained control of the provinces was to pay the other ten million pesos.

Most Peruvians had never reconciled themselves to accepting what they considered an onerous treaty and an abuse of victory in war. They felt that it was the result of a Carthaginian peace, imposed by brute force upon a broken and disunited nation. This feeling resulted in the growth of a strong *revanche* movement, the goal of which was revision of the hated treaty and recovery of the "lost" provinces. The

[1] For the complete text, see Great Britain, Foreign Office, *British and Foreign State Papers, 1882–1883,* LXXIV, 349–53; *Foreign Relations, 1883,* pp. 731–33. For a discussion of the treaty, see Victor A. Belaunde, *The Treaty of Ancón in the Light of International Law.*

[2] The literature on the war is voluminous. A good historical account is Diego Barros Arana, *Historia de la Guerra del Pacífico.* For the role of the United States in the conflict, see the recent account by Herbert Millington, *American Diplomacy and the War of the Pacific.*

Peruvian fervor for retribution was held in check and failed to pro-
duce an armed conflict only because of Chile's naval and military
superiority.[3] Another rankling wound to Peru's national pride was
that the treaty provision regarding the plebiscite had never been carried out. Though the provinces were formerly a part of Peru, Chile
was desirous of retaining them as possible sources of mineral wealth,
and as buffer areas between itself and its vengeful northern neighbor.
With this in mind, Chile attempted a thorough "Chileanization"[4] of
the disputed territory, and carried on a campaign of intimidation
against the luckless Peruvians in the area.

Through the years this "Alsace-Lorraine of South America" em-
bittered relations between the two republics of the Pacific, and for long
periods diplomatic intercourse between them remained suspended.[5]
In addition, they were subject to periodic attacks of "war nerves,"
manifested in economic boycotts and jingoistic newspaper columns
and these antagonisms were nurtured on heroic legends of the war.
Though the disputed land was almost valueless, neither country could
be budged from its intransigent position; the controversy had become
one of honor, and patriotism demanded that the national prestige be
maintained.[6]

Down to World War I, only occasional half-hearted attempts
were made to pierce the curtain of mutual animosity. Not until December 12, 1921, when Chile took the initiative and suggested to Peru
that a plebiscite be held, was the way paved for an ultimate agreement.[7] The defeat of Germany and the successful operation of the
Panama Canal acted as spurs to the development of shipping on the
west coast of South America. Chile was in an advantageous position
to profit from this new development but was seriously hampered by
Peruvian hostility, and was therefore eager to clear up its Peruvian
relations. After prolonged negotiations, the two states agreed to
submit their problem to an arbitration by the United States. Soon

[3] See Cecil Jane, "The Question of Tacna-Arica," *Transactions of the Grotius
Society*, XV (1929), 94, 99.

[4] See Graham H. Stuart, *The Tacna-Arica Dispute*, World Peace Foundation
Pamphlets, Vol. X (1927), No. 1, pp. 33–34.

[5] For a thorough study of the entire Tacna-Arica problem and its diplomacy,
see William J. Dennis, *Tacna and Arica*. For a shorter treatment see Gordon Ireland, *Boundaries, Possessions, and Conflicts in South America*, pp. 160–75. Hereafter cited as Ireland, *South American Boundary Conflicts*.

[6] See Jane, *op. cit.*, p. 98; *Foreign Relations, 1929*, I, 767.

[7] For text of telegram, see Chile, *Tacna-Arica Arbitration. The Appendix to
the Case of the Republic of Chile*, pp. 536–38.

after, in January 1922, President Harding invited both parties to send delegates to Washington to thrash out their problem. Bolivia protested loudly at being excluded, but both Peru and Chile, who had accepted Harding's invitation, refused to include her in the discussions. Negotiations began in the middle of May in Washington, resulting in a protocol of arbitration, signed on July 20, 1922, whereby the two powers agreed to submit their case to the President of the United States as arbitrator. Harding accepted the role.[8]

Finally, after a bitter campaign of charges and countercharges, both powers presented their cases, and on March 4, 1925, President Coolidge, who inherited the task with the presidency, handed down a lengthy award.[9] In the decision, Coolidge favored holding the plebiscite and made provision for the establishment of a three-member commission, with the member from the United States the chairman, to supervise the election.

Since Chile's main contention, that the plebiscite should be held, had been sustained, the decision was received with joyous approval in that country; the Archbishop of Santiago even had the city's church bells sounded as a sign of national rejoicing.[10] But in Lima black gloom prevailed; the award was looked upon as a national calamity. Public dissatisfaction reached alarming proportions. Coolidge's announcement was followed by a general strike, which suspended vehicular traffic, shut down factories and shops, and left the city without newspapers. Demonstrations denouncing the decision occurred daily, and the police were hard put to maintain order. Anti–United States feeling was intense. One crowd of angry rioters mobbed the American embassy and succeeded in demolishing its coat of arms. In fear of further mob violence, the embassy was placed under a special guard of Peruvian soldiers. Similar hostile sentiment prevailed in other sections of the country, and a revolutionary coup against the government was attempted, but was quickly stamped out.

Despite her extreme disappointment over the award, Peru reluctantly accepted it, and the plebiscitary commission, of which Gen-

[8] For the text of the protocol, see *Foreign Relations, 1922*, I, 505–7. See also *New York Times*, January 21, 1922; Chile, *Tacna-Arica Arbitration. The Appendix to the Case of the Republic of Chile;* Peru, *Arbitration Between Peru and Chile. The Countercase of Peru.*

[9] See *New York Times*, March 6, 1925; *ibid.*, March 10, 1925. For complete text, see *Foreign Relations, 1925*, I, 305–60. For Spanish and English text, see Chile, *Tacna-Arica. Fallo arbitral.*

[10] *New York Times*, March 10, 1925.

eral John J. Pershing was made chairman, began its task on August 5, 1925.[11] After almost six months of work, the ground was prepared for the plebiscite, but in the meanwhile old wounds were reopened. A bitter press war raged between the two powers, and disorder reigned in the disputed area.[12] Conditions became so bad that General Pershing was accused by a Chilean official of partiality and of "frustrating the plebiscite."[13] Soon after, Pershing resigned, ostensibly because of his ill-health which had been aggravated by the strain of the proceedings, and returned to the United States.[14] He was replaced by Major General William Lassiter, who soon became convinced that an impartial and honest plebiscite could not be held.[15] He strongly censured terroristic Chilean conduct in the provinces and brought about the termination of the plebiscitary proceedings.[16]

The United States made another unsuccessful attempt to cut the Gordian knot at the end of 1926, when Secretary of State Kellogg suggested a solution that would have given Tacna and Arica to a third interested and land-locked power, Bolivia. Peru refused categorically to consider this solution; Chile indicated an acceptance in principle; only Bolivia found this solution wholly acceptable.[17] But Kellogg was finally able to break the stalemate in July 1928 when he persuaded the two powers to resume diplomatic relations after a lapse of eighteen years. This led to a growth of better feeling between the old enemies, a prerequisite for an adequate settlement. Secretary Kellogg had also suggested that they try to resolve their differences by direct negotiation. This was done after diplomatic relations were formally resumed in October 1928.[18] Thus, considerable progress had been made toward an eventual settlement when Hoover visited Chile and Peru in December of that year.

In the course of his journey, Hoover held discussions on the

---

[11] *Foreign Relations, 1925,* I, 369.

[12] See *New York Times,* March 26, 1925.

[13] *Ibid.,* November 30, 1925.

[14] *Ibid.,* December 30, 1925. Secretary of State Kellogg found it necessary to insist that the only reason for Pershing's return was his health. Apparently the general's dental condition affected his blood pressure; *ibid.,* January 1, 1926.

[15] *Ibid.,* January 13, 1926; *Foreign Relations, 1926,* I, 367–68.

[16] Lassiter's statement, outlining his reasons for the termination, is given in Sarah Wambaugh, *Plebiscites Since the World War,* II, 468–90. In Volume I, 331–410, she relates the entire problem of the attempted plebiscite.

[17] For the text of the note, see *Foreign Relations, 1926,* I, 504–9; for Chile's attitude, *ibid.,* pp. 512–15; for Peru's rejection, *ibid.,* pp. 520–30; for Bolivia's acceptance, *ibid.,* pp. 510–11.

[18] *Foreign Relations, 1928,* I, 663–65.

vexatious subject with President Augusto B. Leguía of Peru, President Carlos Ibáñez of Chile, and with the minister for foreign affairs of Bolivia, Alberto Palacios, who paid him a special visit on the U.S.S. *Maryland*, while it was anchored off Antofagasta, Chile.[19] From these talks Hoover was able to ascertain the grounds upon which the political leaders of these countries would be willing to discuss settlement of the thorny question. To his surprise, he found that both Chile and Peru were now ready to concede more than was necessary to solve the enigma of half a century.[20] From his personal understandings with the parties concerned, it was then a comparatively simple matter for the President-elect to propose an acceptable solution.

Although both Chile and Peru agreed in principle on the proposed settlement, Hoover found that there were still some minor difficulties in the way of a complete understanding. Consequently, he promised, as a friend of both parties, that he would take action to promote a final agreement when he assumed office.[21] Soon after his inauguration, President Hoover put into motion the necessary machinery to carry out his promise effectively. The Department of State worked feverishly to bring about a quick and complete agreement, as Secretary Kellogg was extremely anxious to reach a settlement before he left office.[22] In the delicate drama of these closing negotiations, conducted by the State Department, Alexander P. Moore, United States ambassador to Peru, and William S. Culbertson, ambassador to Chile, played important parts. Even in its last stages, the problem was still exasperating for the negotiators. In a dispatch to Secretary of State Stimson, Moore referred to the antics of Peru and Chile as similar to those "of two bald-headed men fighting over a comb." He found that the most persistent obstacle to a "really practical and economic settlement" was still the touchy pride of the two powers.[23]

After the proper diplomatic legalities had been completed by the Department of State, and both parties had agreed on the draft of the final proposal, President Hoover submitted to Chile and Peru on May 14, 1929, "the final bases of the solution" of the long-standing "question of the Pacific." He acted not as arbitrator but as a neutral party exercising his good offices at the request of both disputants.[24]

[19] See *New York Times*, December 9, 1928; *Hoover's Latin-American Addresses*, p. 24.

[20] Hoover interview, August 5, 1947.

[21] *Foreign Relations, 1929*, I, 803; *New York Times*, May 18, 1929.

[22] *Foreign Relations, 1929*, I, 732.

[23] *Ibid.*, p. 767.   [24] *Ibid.*, p. 803.

His proposal was a revised summary of the points agreed upon in direct negotiations between the principals.[25] Hoover's proposal was forthwith accepted by the two governments and transformed into a treaty concluded on June 3, 1929. The treaty was ratified by both governments, and the exchange of ratifications took place on July 28, 1929.[26]

Except for an additional protocol aimed at Bolivian aspirations, the treaty embodied all of Hoover's proposals. The major provisions of the treaty were that the disputed territory was divided into two parts, Tacna going to Peru and Arica to Chile. Chile was to give Peru six million dollars, grant her free-port privileges in the Bay of Arica, a customhouse, and a railroad station. In addition, Chile was to turn over all public works and government-owned property in Tacna to Peru without cost. To commemorate the agreement, the two nations agreed to erect a monument on the Morro de Arica.

The settlement was well received by the majority of the people of both Chile and Peru and brought about "a rich harvest of good will for the United States."[27] Most other countries praised the settlement. Brazil's president wired Hoover his congratulations,[28] the Council of the League of Nations lauded the work of the United States, and even Argentina praised the role of Uncle Sam. Bolivia expressed dissatisfaction with the settlement, which left her shut off from free access to the sea. As an interested party, and the only land-locked nation of Latin America, she had expected to gain some advantages from the settlement. In his proposal, Hoover took pains to show that nothing stood in the way of Bolivia's taking up the question of her access to the sea directly with Chile or Peru.[29]

Hoover's last official act in connection with the Tacna-Arica affair was his final ruling as arbitrator, succeeding Coolidge, on August 2, 1929, whereby he terminated the proceedings begun under Harding in 1922. Thus was removed from the field of controversy an aggravating problem that had for approximately half a century hung like a cloud over the international relations of the South American con-

[25] See Stimson to Culbertson, May 10, 1929, *Foreign Relations, 1929*, I, 796; for the memorandum of Chile and Peru, *ibid.*, p. 798.

[26] *Ibid.*, p. 812.

[27] Hoover Papers, Culbertson to Hoover, May 13, 1929.

[28] *New York Times*, May 22, 1929; also editorial, *ibid.*, May 20, 1929.

[29] See Stimson's statement, *ibid.*, May 19, 1929. He said that the settlement made possible an adjustment whereby Bolivia could acquire an outlet on the Pacific; *ibid.*, May 18, 1929.

tinent. Many Americans had taken an honorable part in trying to unravel the tangled situation, but not until Hoover's visit to Latin America, and his co-operation in suggesting a solution, was a final settlement possible.[30] Henry L. Stimson, who had an intimate knowledge of this affair, called it "Mr. Hoover's greatest personal triumph" in the field of conciliation and arbitration.[31]

On several other occasions during his administration President Hoover was able to extend the good offices of the government in behalf of Latin-American countries. He emphasized this function in his message to Congress on December 10, 1931, when he declared that "it has been the privilege of this government to lend its good offices on several occasions in the past to the settlement of boundary disputes between the American republics."[32] An outgrowth of the efforts of the administration in this field was the settlement of the hundred-year-old boundary dispute between Guatemala and Honduras.[33]

This dispute, as was true of most Latin-American boundary controversies, had its antecedents in the early period of independence from Spain.[34] Soon after the Central American Federation was dissolved in 1842, differences over their boundary cropped up between Guatemala and Honduras. From 1847 onwards, a number of unsuccessful attempts were made by both countries to resolve their differences.[35] The situation did not become threatening until 1915, when the activities of two rival American-owned companies collided, resulting in some armed skirmishes in 1917.[36] In this conflict, Honduras backed the Cuyamel Fruit Company, to whom it had granted

[30] Hoover Papers, Alexander P. Moore to Hoover, May 3, 1929. Moore maintained that "it was only your visit to South America that made this settlement possible." Also Moore to Hoover, June 7, 1929.

[31] Henry L. Stimson and McGeorge Bundy, *On Active Service in Peace and War*, p. 185. Hereafter referred to as Stimson and Bundy, *On Active Service*.

[32] William S. Myers, ed., *The State Papers and Other Public Writings of Herbert Hoover*, II, 79. Hereafter cited as Myers, ed., *Hoover Papers*.

[33] For a well-documented historical summary of this dispute, see Gordon Ireland, *Boundaries, Possessions, and Conflicts in Central and North America and the Caribbean*, pp. 86–94 (hereafter referred to as Ireland, *Central American Boundary Disputes*); see also Chester L. Jones, *Guatemala Past and Present*, pp. 85–88; Toynbee, *International Affairs, 1930*, pp. 439–40; Guatemala, Ministry of Foreign Affairs, *The Boundary Dispute Between Guatemala and Honduras*. For the Honduran side, see Eduardo Martínez López, *Honduras y Guatemala: Límites*.

[34] Guatemala, *Arbitraje de límites entre Guatemala y Honduras; alegato presentado por Guatemala . . . .*, pp. 3 ff.

[35] Ireland, *op. cit.*, pp. 86–89.

[36] See *Foreign Relations, 1917*, pp. 760 ff.

concessions and land in the disputed area, while the United Fruit Company received support from the Guatemalan government as the result of similar grants.

Both countries sent troops into the frontier territory, and Honduras appealed to the United States, which exercised its good offices to prevent further conflict. The American government then offered to act as mediator, and asked the two parties to send delegates to Washington to work out a solution. This boundary conference first met in 1918, with both sides presenting their claims in detail.[37] An economic survey was made of the disputed region in an effort to find an equitable boundary line, but failed to settle the issue. In 1923 at the Washington Conference on Central American affairs, the two nations decided to submit their cases to an arbitration by the President of the United States. Nothing came of this, however, as the arbitration was not held. In 1927 new incidents again threatened war, and the United States vainly attempted to reconcile the differences of the two powers by mediation at Cuyamel, Honduras, in April 1928. It failed even to establish a provisional boundary line. In June of the same year, Secretary of State Kellogg proposed that the case be brought before the International Central American Tribunal, which had been established by a convention signed in Washington, in February 1923. Guatemala accepted this proposal, but Honduras rejected it. Discussions continued, but with no solution in sight.

Finally, on October 25, 1929, Secretary of State Stimson informed the governments of Guatemala and Honduras that the United States "felt that the discussion regarding disputes between these countries had reached a point where further progress could best be realized by a frank and friendly exchange of views in Washington."[38] Invitations were extended to both governments to send representatives to Washington, and the State Department offered its aid in the discussions. By November, both parties accepted.

Officials from the two countries met in Washington on January 20, 1930. At first the two governments stubbornly stood their ground. They disagreed over who should be asked to arbitrate and whether or not the International Central American Tribunal had jurisdiction in the matter. After considerable negotiations the State Department suggested, by way of compromise, that a special tribunal be created.

[37] See *Foreign Relations, 1919*, I, 85–114.
[38] Department of State Press Releases, No. 7 (November 12, 1929), p. 63; also *Foreign Relations, 1929*, I, 963–64.

After concessions by both sides, the proposal was accepted. This led to the signing of a treaty on July 16, 1930, which prepared the way for the final settlement.[39] Under its terms both Guatemala and Honduras agreed to submit the question of the boundary dispute to arbitration. In addition there was signed a supplementary convention, providing for the delimitation of the boundary after the arbitral tribunal should hand down its award.[40]

The Special Boundary tribunal, presided over by Chief Justice Charles E. Hughes of the United States Supreme Court, held its first meeting on December 15, 1931, and on January 23, 1933, handed down its opinion and award.[41] The decision, based essentially on the status quo of actual occupation, divided the disputed area between the parties. The treaty and its results met with approval in both countries, though it was at first received with some disappointment in Honduras. There was a general feeling of relief evident in the two republics after this century-old controversy had at last been peacefully settled.

[39] Department of State, "Review of Questions of Major Interest in the Relations of the United States with the Latin American Countries, 1929–1933," Part III (unpublished). Hereafter referred to as Department of State, "Review of Questions." See also F. C. Fisher, "The Arbitration of the Guatemalan-Honduran Boundary Dispute," *American Journal of International Law,* XXVII (July 1933), 410; also *Foreign Relations, 1930,* I, 344–61.

[40] Department of State, "Review of Questions," Part III.

[41] *Ibid.*; also *New York Times,* January 24, 1933. For the text in English and Spanish, see Special Boundary Tribunal (Guatemala-Honduras Boundary Arbitration), *Opinion and Award.*

CHAPTER IV

TRYING TO KEEP THE PEACE

"I have projected a new doctrine into international affairs, the doctrine that we do not and never will recognize title to possession of territory gained in violation of the peace pacts. That doctrine has been accepted by all the nations of the world . . . . and . . . . by all the nations of the Western Hemisphere."
—President Hoover, 1932

The Hoover administration offered the use of its good offices to several Latin-American countries in two other disputes that threatened the peace of the Western Hemisphere. Though neither of these controversies was settled until after Hoover was out of office, his government made persistent attempts to reach settlements that were fair to all concerned.

It was in reference to the Chaco affair between Bolivia and Paraguay and the Leticia dispute between Peru and Colombia that the "Hoover-Stimson doctrine" was most widely quoted, though it was better known for its application in Manchuria. The essence of this doctrine was that the United States would not recognize any situation, treaty, or agreement, which might be brought about in violation of peace treaties. Though this policy of not recognizing the fruits of aggression was not new in Latin-American diplomacy, it was unique in that it was adopted by Hoover as a basis for United States foreign policy, and in that it came to be accepted by most of the world.[1] Hoover did not claim credit for originating the formula; in fact, he admitted that he got the idea from William Jennings Bryan, a former Secretary of State, who used it in reference to the open-door policy in China.[2] The doctrine was first applied during the Hoover administration by Secretary of State Henry L. Stimson on January 7, 1932, when he sent identical notes to Japan and China, protesting the Japa-

[1] For the text of the doctrine, see Department of State Press Releases, No. 119 (January 9, 1932), pp. 41–42. See also H. Lauterpacht, *Recognition in International Law*, p. 417.

[2] Statement by Mr. Hoover in personal interview of August 5, 1947. For Bryan's use of the formula, see his note of March 11, 1915, to Japan and China in *Foreign Relations, 1915*, p. 146. See also Graham H. Stuart, *The Department of State*, p. 305.

nese invasion of Manchuria.[3] These notes contained the text of the doctrine and, as a consequence, much of the credit for the nonrecognition principle has been given to Stimson, though in his memoirs he gave Hoover full credit for its adoption.[4] The Hoover-Stimson doctrine had little effect in curtailing aggression in the Far East, but it did receive world-wide approval and was adopted by the republics of the Western Hemisphere. It was applied to the Chaco conflict with limited success.

The Chaco controversy was the result of a boundary dispute between Bolivia and Paraguay over an extensive wilderness, known as the Chaco Boreal.[5] The rival claims traced their origins back to the colonial period, with both countries able to construct strong cases: Bolivia by title and Paraguay through possession.[6] American intercession on behalf of peace also had an early beginning. In November 1878, President Rutherford B. Hayes settled a boundary disagreement between Argentina and Paraguay when he handed down an arbitral award favorable to Paraguay. Bolivia protested, as she felt her claims in the region were not recognized.[7]

For years Paraguay and Bolivia were in disagreement over this jungle area. Little was done toward bringing about a real agreement concerning a frontier line acceptable to both. There were some half-hearted efforts at settlement, but the basic dissension remained. After Bolivia was ignominiously defeated in the War of the Pacific (1879–1883) and lost her Pacific Ocean coast line to Chile, the dominant

---

[3] See *Foreign Relations, Japan, 1931–1941*, I, 76; see also Quincy Wright, "The Stimson Note of January 7, 1932," *American Journal of International Law*, XXVI (April 1932), 342–48.

[4] See Stimson and Bundy, *On Active Service*, pp. 234 and 244. Hoover thought that "the note would take rank with the greatest papers of this century." See also Myers, ed., *Hoover Papers*, II, 260. Hoover acknowledged responsibility for the doctrine. Statement by Mr. Hoover in a personal interview, August 5, 1947.

[5] For descriptions of the Chaco and a historical summary of the dispute, see Ireland, *South American Boundary Conflicts*, pp. 66–95; John C. De Wilde, "South American Conflicts: The Chaco and Leticia," *Foreign Policy Reports*, IX (May 24, 1933), 57–68; William L. Schurz, "The Chaco Dispute Between Bolivia and Paraguay," *Foreign Affairs*, VII (July 1929), 650–55; Toynbee, *International Affairs, 1930*, pp. 421–36; *ibid., 1933*, pp. 393–438; League of Nations, Chaco Commission, *Dispute Between Bolivia and Paraguay*, chaps. i and ii. This is an authoritative report by the Chaco Commission.

[6] For the rival claims based on colonial antecedents, see José Aguirre Achá, *La antigua provincia de Chiquitos;* Manuel Domínguez, *Seven Kings and Ten Viceroys Affirm the Rights of Paraguay Over the Chaco.*

[7] For the text of the award, see *Foreign Relations, 1878–1879*, p. 711. For Bolivia's protest, see León M. Loza, *El laudo Hayes*, pp. 64–79.

theme of her foreign policy became the acquisition of an unobstructed outlet to the sea. This gave new impetus to Bolivian designs on the Chaco, from where, if her claims were successful, she could reach the Atlantic via the Pilcomayo and Paraguay rivers. Her hopes for regaining a port on the Pacific were shattered by the Tacna-Arica settlement, as both Chile and Peru chose to ignore her claims. Thus her plans for a port became focused on the Chaco and the Atlantic. But here Bolivia found an alert rival in Paraguay. Argentina, reluctant to have another flag on the Paraguay river, supported Paraguay. Chile, on the other hand, anxious to divert Bolivian resentment, encouraged her efforts. Argentina had attempted to reconcile the two rivals in 1927, after a series of incidents on the frontier, but her efforts were in vain.

This was the situation up to December 1928, when Hoover set out on his good-will tour. Even while Hoover was meeting high government officials from Bolivia and Chile and working for a solution to the Tacna-Arica problem, serious clashes took place between Paraguayan and Bolivian forces at an isolated Bolivian outpost in the Chaco. War fever rose in both countries, but fortunately the International Conference of American States on Conciliation and Arbitration was about to begin its sessions in Washington. The first act of the assembled delegates was to offer to the two countries the good offices of the conference and to appoint a special committee, composed of representatives from the United States and four Latin-American states, to study the situation, so that steps might be taken to settle the affair.[8] Through Secretary of State Stimson, who was chairman of the gathering, the offer was accepted, and a Commission of Conciliation was formed, composed of two members, each, from Bolivia and Paraguay, plus delegates from the United States, Colombia, Cuba, Mexico, and Uruguay.

This commission began its work in March 1929, soon after Hoover assumed office, and by September it succeeded in bringing about a peaceful settlement of the frontier incidents that was satisfactory to both parties. The accord was based on the restoration of the status quo prior to December 1928 and a resumption of diplomatic relations. But as the fundamental question, which the commission was not empowered to handle, was not settled, the situation was still fraught with danger. With this in mind, the commissioners from the neutral countries proposed in August 1930 an arbitration

[8] Department of State, "Review of Questions," Part II, pp. 2–3.

through the good offices of their respective countries; and the United States offered its facilities in Washington for the negotiations.[9] Paraguay accepted the suggestion, but Bolivia indicated a preference for direct negotiations.

Conditions were further complicated by a revolution in the latter part of June 1930, which caused a change in Bolivia's government. Paraguay took the position that until a constitutional government was formed in Bolivia, further negotiations could not be carried on. But in the first part of 1931, soon after the restoration of a constitutional government, Bolivia accepted the offer of the five neutrals and reluctantly consented to consider the conclusion of a nonaggression pact.[10] Paraguay accepted this proposal, but before peace talks could begin a new clash increased the friction between the hostile powers, and Bolivia balked at the renewal of the negotiations.[11]

As a result of the efforts of the neutrals this skirmish had no serious consequences, and in November 1931 parleys began under the auspices of the five neutral governments, organized as a Commission of Neutrals, with Assistant Secretary of State Francis White as chairman. After six months of considering numerous proposals and counterproposals, a nonaggression pact was drawn up by the delegates in May 1932.[12] While the discussions were going on, hostilities broke out anew. The seriousness of the dissension caused grave concern in the neighboring states of Brazil, Chile, Peru, and particularly in Argentina, whose economic interests were endangered. Anxiety led these powers to agree to co-operate with the Commission of Neutrals.

After conferring with Brazil, Chile, Peru, and Argentina, the neutrals, on the initiative of Chairman White, requested all of the American republics to apply collectively the Hoover-Stimson doctrine to the Chaco dispute.[13] In prompt compliance, on August 3, 1932, the nineteen nations of the Pan American Union (all except Bolivia and Paraguay) dispatched a joint telegraphic appeal to the quarreling states, calling upon them to cease troop movements im-

[9] *Ibid.*, pp. 8–10.

[10] *Ibid.*, pp. 13–14; see also *Foreign Relations, 1931,* I, 715, 748–49.

[11] Department of State, "Review of Questions," Part II, p. 16; De Wilde, *op. cit.,* p. 61.

[12] Department of State, "Review of Questions," Part II, pp. 18–25; *New York Times,* May 31, 1932; see also *Foreign Relations,* 1931, I, 770–71.

[13] Department of State, "Review of Questions," Part II, pp. 28–30; see also *New York Times,* January 1, 1933, II, 6.

mediately and to present their respective cases to the Commission of Neutrals. The appeal closed with the warning that "the American nations further declare that they will not recognize any territorial arrangement of this controversy which has not been obtained by peaceful means nor the validity of territorial acquisitions which may be obtained through occupation or conquest by force of arms."[14] Supported by this declaration of unity, the Commission of Neutrals worked hard to heal the rupture, but reached an impasse, since neither side would compromise its stand. Paraguay's reply indicated an acceptance of the conditions in the dispatch, but Bolivia, though expressing agreement with the principle of the doctrine, maintained that the Chaco was Bolivian, and therefore the doctrine had no application in this case.[15]

During the course of the controversy, the League of Nations had kept a watchful eye on the situation. At first, League policy had been opposed to intervention in the dispute, in view of the mediatory action under way by the American states. Its officials followed a policy of keeping the United States informed of the League's relations with the disputants, since they could not wholly ignore a situation such as this between member states. But when the strife became acute, the League overcame its hesitancy. In September 1932 the Council of the League of Nations appointed a small committee to follow developments in the disagreement and offered its co-operation to the Commission of Neutrals.

In October and November more sparring took place in the Chaco, and it finally developed into open warfare. A detailed proposal by the neutral American states, supported by the League, was made to the belligerents on December 15, 1932. It embraced not only suspension of hostilities, but the basis for arbitration and for the settlement of the main problem. Two days later the proposal was rejected by Paraguay. Independent proposals by Chile and other nations were also refused. Then, in January 1933, the League committee proposed sending a three-member commission to the Chaco. This was opposed by the Department of State, because it felt that the new commission would complicate the work of other peace agencies now in progress.[16] A few months later, after Hoover was out of office, Paraguay declared war on Bolivia.

[14] For the full text, see Department of State Press Releases, No. 149 (August 6, 1932), pp. 98–101.
[15] Department of State, "Review of Questions," Part II, pp. 31–35.
[16] Ibid., pp. 39–46.

The fourth Latin-American conflict in which the Hoover administration became involved was that between Peru and Colombia following a flare-up of hostilities in the almost inaccessible Amazon river port of Leticia.[17] This controversy came to a climax in the twilight of Hoover's presidential term, and was finally settled peaceably through the efforts of the United States, the League of Nations, and Brazil. In the controversy, Secretary of State Stimson found it necessary to remind Peru several times of the sanction imposed by the Hoover-Stimson doctrine; and the League of Nations, with the full support of the United States, invoked this doctrine against Peru with success.[18]

Although less complicated than the Chaco dispute, this affair was potentially even more dangerous. It threatened to involve other powers, namely Brazil and Ecuador, if it developed into a full-fledged shooting war. The seeds of the disagreement were sown in the period of the Spanish vice-royalities, but its modern beginning stemmed from the Salomón-Lozano Treaty between Peru and Colombia, which was signed in 1922 and executed in 1930.[19] Ostensibly this treaty had settled finally and irrevocably the long-standing boundary difficulty in the Leticia area between the two republics. Even before the treaty had been ratified by either country, the United States became an interested party in the problem. Brazil had objected to the treaty as injurious to her interests, and at Colombia's request Secretary of State Hughes took up the matter with Brazil. After extended negotiations, a *procès-verbal*, arranging for tripartite boundary settlements between Brazil, Colombia, and Peru, was drawn up under the good offices of Hughes and was signed by the three parties shortly before he left his position in the cabinet in March 1925.[20]

Local feeling in the Peruvian frontier department of Loreto was antagonistic to the treaty settlement, and was opposed to the transfer of any part of the area to Colombia. This animosity flamed into action

[17] For the history of this dispute, see Alfonso Mejía Robledo, *Los piratas del Amazonas;* also Council of the League of Nations, *Dispute Between Colombia and Peru* (hereafter cited as League, *Colombia and Peru*); Ireland, *South American Boundary Conflicts*, pp. 196–206; De Wilde, *op. cit.*, pp. 66–68; and Toynbee, *op. cit., 1933*, pp. 438–57.

[18] League, *Colombia and Peru*, p. 12.

[19] For a Peruvian discussion of the treaty, see Evaristo San Cristóval, *Páginas internacionales*, pp. 105–37; for text of treaty, *ibid.*, pp. 139–43. For a Colombian viewpoint, see Antonio José Uribe, *Colombia y el Perú*, pp. 140–46.

[20] For the text of the agreement, see *Foreign Relations, 1925*, I, 461–63; for negotiations, see *ibid.*, p. 436 ff.; see also Department of State, "Review of Questions," Part II, p. 1.

on September 1, 1932, when an armed band of about three hundred Peruvians seized the Colombian town of Leticia, expelled its officials, and raised the Peruvian flag.[21] The President of Peru, Luis M. Sánchez Cerro, labeled the invaders as Communists and as Apristas, his chief political opponents. He privately informed Colombia that he would do everything possible to keep the incident from becoming serious and disclaimed responsibility for the episode. But when pressed for a public disavowal by United States Ambassador Fred M. Dearing, he refused.[22]

Local Peruvian authorities furnished the filibusters military support. Late in November Peruvian regular troops occupied Leticia. In the meanwhile the Colombian government, with the purpose of regaining and restoring order in its invaded territory, armed a small flotilla of six vessels, which proceeded toward Leticia from the Atlantic and thence up the 2,500 miles of the Amazon river. Stopping at several Brazilian river ports along the way, the expedition finally reached Colombian territorial waters on or about February 12, 1933.[23] Previously apathetic Peruvian public opinion now became aroused over the expedition, which was looked upon as being punitive and aggressive, and demanded that the government protect its citizens. The war spirit in both countries rose rapidly, and patriotic appeals and nationalistic propaganda of the governments prepared the minds of their people for war.[24]

Actual hostilities began when the Colombian flotilla, on the day of its arrival in the contested area, was attacked by Peruvian aircraft, which in turn were successfully counterattacked by Colombian planes. A few days later the Colombian expedition assaulted and captured the town of Tarapacá, which the Peruvian intruders had occupied after their initial attack. As a result of this encounter, Peru and Colombia severed diplomatic relations on February 15, 1933.[25]

Long before the controversy had reached the shooting stage, the United States tried to end the dissension. On September 13, 1932, Secretary of State Stimson spoke personally to the Peruvian ambas-

[21] League, *Colombia and Peru,* p. 2; Department of State, "Review of Questions," II, 1; *New York Times,* September 4, 1932.

[22] Department of State, Review of Questions," Part II, pp. 2–3.

[23] See League, *Colombia and Peru,* p. 2; Toynbee, *op. cit., 1933,* p. 447.

[24] Department of State, "Review of Questions," Part II, p. 6; *New York Times,* September 20 to 22, 1932; *ibid.,* October 2, 4, and 30, 1932. War chests had been raised by both countries.

[25] League, *Colombia and Peru,* p. 3; Ireland, *South American Boundary Conflicts,* pp. 200–201.

sador in Washington, reminding him that treaties should be respected. He alluded to the inconsistency between Peru's position with respect to Leticia and its solemn adherence, with the other American nations, to the Hoover-Stimson doctrine a month before, when it was applied to the Chaco dispute.[26] The Peruvian government soon changed its attitude toward the disagreement and began characterizing the Loretano movement as "nationalistic" and motivated by patriotism. Ambassador Dearing found evidence that the movement was not Communist or Aprista inspired but was directed solely against Colombia.[27] Up to this time the Colombian press and public opinion had taken the incident calmly, but with the Peruvian attitude disclosed, anti-Peruvian feeling rose to a high pitch in Bogotá.

With the object of getting a favorable revision of the 1922 treaty and the Colombian boundary, Peru, on October 3, 1932, appealed to the Permanent Commission on Inter-American Conciliation at Washington, D.C., to inquire into the whole affair.[28] This request was forwarded to Colombia, which held that the problem was purely a domestic one, concerning only Colombian territory, and that domestic issues were not subject to the purview of the commission. This attitude was backed by Colombian public opinion, which would not permit the question of sovereignty over Colombian territory to be submitted to a conciliation commission. Colombia, however, informed Peru that it would willingly discuss any grievances concerning the boundary treaty, but only after its authority in the Leticia area had been restored.[29] Peru rejected this condition.

Ecuador had expressed her interest in the affair, and in the middle of November 1932 notified all the American countries that her interests could not be ignored in any settlement of the Leticia territory.[30] Except for a number of informal attempts by the United States to maintain the peace, which proved fruitless, there were few new developments through November and the early part of December. But in the last days of December, another neutral party, Brazil, became

[26] Department of State, "Review of Questions," Part II, p. 5.

[27] Ibid., pp. 6–7.

[28] Ibid., pp. 9–10; Ireland, South American Boundary Conflicts, p. 198; New York Times, October 6, 1932, and January 13, 1933.

[29] Department of State, "Review of Questions," Part II, p. 10; New York Times, October 14, 1932.

[30] Department of State, "Review of Questions," Part II, p. 11; see also Manuel Cabeza de Vaca, La posición del Ecuador en el conflicto colombo-peruano; Toynbee, op. cit., 1933, pp. 442–43; New York Times, November 15, 1932, and December 31, 1932.

alarmed, and believing an armed clash imminent, offered to mediate the dispute.[31] This offer received the full support of the United States, which had earlier tried to get Brazil to play a more dominant role in the efforts to settle the question peaceably.[32] Colombia immediately embraced the Brazilian proposal, but Peru would not. On January 10, 1933, Ambassador Dearing was instructed to urge the Peruvian government to accept the Brazilian suggestion and to point out that Peru's support of the Leticia invaders was a violation of the Kellogg-Briand Peace Pact. Several days later Peru replied by labeling Colombia as the aggressor and maintaining that "in Loreto the desire exists that the Colombian authorities shall not return to Leticia."[33]

At this point the League of Nations approached both Colombia and Peru (the situation had been brought to the attention of the League earlier by Colombia), expressing the desire that they would abide by their obligations as League members. About two weeks later, on January 23, 1933, Peru requested the Council of the League "to order the suspension of all measures of force" in the dispute.[34] On that same day, Colombia appealed to the United States and to the other signatories of the Kellogg-Briand Anti-War Pact, calling attention to Peru's violation of her sovereignty and the disregard for treaty obligations, and requesting that Peru be reminded of those obligations.

The next day, Secretary Stimson held a conference at his home in Washington with the representatives of the leading signatories of the pact—France, Great Britain, Germany, Italy, and Japan—informing them of the action the United States proposed to take in the Leticia issue and urging them to have their governments take similar action.[35] He followed this by sending a comprehensive note to Peru, indicating that her support of the Loretanos would be a violation of the peace pact, and urged that government to accept the Brazilian peace formula. He closed with a reference to the Hoover-Stimson doctrine, to which Peru had adhered in August 1932. A copy of the note was sent to the secretary general of the League of Nations.[36]

For a while a conflict of jurisdiction seemed probable, but both

[31] Department of State, "Review of Questions," Part II, p. 13; see *New York Times,* January 22, 1933; for Brazil's role in the affair, see Jayme de Barros, *Ocho años de política exterior del Brasil,* pp. 29–34.

[32] Department of State, "Review of Questions," Part II, p. 13.

[33] *Ibid.,* pp. 16–20.

[34] League, *Colombia and Peru,* p. 6; *New York Times,* January 24, 1933.

[35] Department of State, "Review of Questions," Part II, pp. 21–22.

[36] For the text, see Department of State Press Releases, No. 174 (January 28, 1931), pp. 66–70.

the United States and the League gave their support to Colombia, and thus both upheld the sanctity of treaties. Peru replied at length to Stimson's note. She announced her intention of complying with the peace pact and the Hoover-Stimson doctrine, but would not relinquish Leticia until she could obtain a modification of the Salomón-Lozano Treaty.[37] To break the stalemate, Colombia, on February 17, 1933, finally invoked Article XV of the League covenant and requested that an extraordinary session be held to deal with the case. The League Council considered the matter on February 21, 1933, and then proposed setting up a commission to settle the situation and to control the disputed area during the period of negotiations.[38]

The secretary general of the League urged Washington to give its support to the proposal at Bogotá and Lima.[39] In prompt compliance with this request, on February 27, 1933, Stimson sent identical notes to Colombia and Peru, stating that he found the proposal suggested by the League "a most straightforward, helpful one, which, if accepted by both parties, should make possible a peaceful solution of the present controversy, honorable to both Governments." He concluded with the statement that "in giving my fullest support to this proposal I have the honor to express the hope that your Government will see its way clear to accepting it."[40] This put to rest any fears that the United States might use the Monroe Doctrine to oppose League efforts to settle disputes in the Western Hemisphere. Thus one of the last acts of the Hoover administration was to support the cause of peace and approve a proposal that brought a League commission to South America.[41]

The United States almost became directly involved in the Leticia controversy on two occasions. The first time was in February 1933, when a mob assaulted, sacked, and attempted to burn the Colombian legation at Lima, and the Colombian minister barely escaped with his life. Ambassador Dearing promptly demanded that Peru provide adequate protection for Americans and the diplomatic corps, and that it take steps to prevent any new mob attacks. He followed this by

[37] Department of State, "Review of Questions," Part II, p. 26.

[38] League, *Colombia and Peru,* pp. 7–8; see *New York Times,* February 19 and 24, 1933.

[39] Department of State, "Review of Questions," Part II, p. 45.

[40] For the complete text of the notes, see Department of State Press Releases, No. 179 (March 4, 1933), p. 159; also contains the substance of the League proposal.

[41] Shortly after Hoover went out of office, the League in its report of March 17, 1933, invoked the Hoover-Stimson doctrine with success and referred to its acceptance by the American nations in August when used in the Chaco dispute; see League, *Colombia and Peru,* p. 12.

making arrangements for the Colombian minister and his family to leave for Ecuador. Because of the evident Peruvian hostility toward Americans, Dearing apparently feared that the Peruvian government would not grant them sufficient protection; he therefore suggested to Washington that a war vessel be sent to Peruvian waters on a friendly visit during the period of uncertainty. The State Department immediately rejected the proposal, declaring that in view of Peru's previous assurances of protection it did not appear that American lives were in danger.[42] In this manner, active intervention was avoided and anti-American hostility soon subsided.

The other case involved the Peruvian cruiser *Bolognesi*, which in January 1933 was reported proceeding to Balboa for the purpose of using the facilities of the Canal Zone dry dock there. The Peruvian ambassador in Washington was advised on January 19 that in cases of possible armed conflict between two American states it was the policy of the United States to refrain from facilitating in any way the preparations of either party. He was then informed, that in view of the ominous condition at Leticia, the use of the dry dock at Balboa would not be available to the cruiser. The policy was expanded the next day, in a letter from the State Department to the War and Navy Departments, denying the use of all United States facilities and any other assistance to Bolivia and Paraguay as well as to Peru and Colombia.[43] This practice was followed throughout the Hoover administration, in addition to the direct use of good offices, which aided considerably the cause of peace south of the border.

[42] Department of State, "Review of Questions," Part II, pp. 41–43; see also *New York Times,* February 21, 1933.

[43] Department of State, "Review of Questions, Part II, pp. 1–2.

CHAPTER V

TAKING THE STING OUT OF
THE MONROE DOCTRINE

"The Monroe Doctrine is not now and never was an instrument of aggression; it is and always has been a cloak of protection. The Doctrine is not a lance; it is a shield."
—FRANK B. KELLOGG, 1929

"The Monroe Doctrine is equivalent to annexing the Continent."
—ALBERTO PALACIOS, 1929

With the advent of Herbert Hoover to the White House there came a marked and deliberate change in the Latin-American policy of the United States.[1] The change is evident in the words and tone of his inaugural address of March 4, 1929, in which he devoted a paragraph specifically to inter-American relations. He referred to the southern continent and his recent trip there in friendly and understanding terms, and assured the southern nations that he wished "only the maintenance of their independence, the growth of their stability, and their prosperity."[2] He also indicated that the Latin-American policy of his administration was to be an integral part of a foreign policy predicated on peace.

To aid him in carrying out this foreign policy, Hoover chose as his Secretary of State Henry L. Stimson, a former close friend of Theodore Roosevelt, and at one time an advocate of the Roosevelt corollary to the Monroe Doctrine.[3] Though admittedly not an expert in the field of international relations, Stimson did have an unusual record of experience in Latin-American affairs.[4] At times the combination of Hoover and Stimson did not function too well, and in the last two years of the administration there was a wide cleavage between the two men

[1] See Toynbee, *International Affairs, 1930,* pp. 361 ff.; Tessan, *Le président Hoover et la politique américaine,* p. 120; William S. Myers and Walter H. Newton, *The Hoover Administration,* p. 531.   [2] Myers, ed., *Hoover Papers,* I, 9–10.
[3] See Stimson and Bundy, *On Active Service,* pp. 155–56. Kellogg would have preferred to have Dwight Morrow succeed him; Bryn-Jones, *Frank B. Kellogg,* p. 184. A few Latins were bitter over the appointment, as they disapproved of Stimson's record in the Philippines; see Palacios, *Nuestra América y el imperialismo yanqui,* p. 108.   [4] Stimson and Bundy, *op. cit.,* p. 157.

45

over foreign policy.[5] But through all of their personal differences on other matters, they were in complete agreement on Latin-American policy. Stimson retained a great admiration for his chief, and profited from Hoover's wide experience in world affairs. With Stimson as his chosen aide, Hoover proceeded to modify the Latin-American policy of his predecessor about as rapidly as one could modify the policy of another President of his own party.[6]

Although in the last two years of the Hoover administration inter-American affairs were overshadowed by portentous events in Europe and Asia and by the great depression at home, "the fundamental purposes and philosophy" of the administration in foreign affairs were to be found in its Latin-American policy.[7] Basic to this policy was the Monroe Doctrine, a pillar of American foreign policy since it was first announced by President James Monroe and his astute Secretary of State, John Quincy Adams. Another essential principle of Latin-American relations, inherited by Hoover, was the *de facto* domination of the Central American and Caribbean area by the United States. In this danger zone the United States has been extremely sensitive to any actual or attempted intervention by any other first-rate power. The region has formed a vital link in American defense strategy for over a century, and since the building of the Panama Canal it has been considered the jugular vein of the American defense system.

The Caribbean area had not been difficult to dominate, as the independent republics in it were small, quarrelsome, and impotent in a world of power politics. As a consequence, the United States had taken every action which seemed consonant with its own national interest and which would prevent other powerful nations from intervening in the affairs of these countries. At times American intervention was pursued in terms of self-interest, but quite often it was carried on under the guise of the Monroe Doctrine—especially since 1904, when Theodore Roosevelt added his famous corollary to this historic document. The interventions and the unilateral interpretation of Monroe's words by the United States stirred up a strong fear and hatred of the northern giant in Latin America.[8] This feeling of re-

---

[5] Stimson and Bundy, *op. cit.*, pp. 195–200.

[6] See William S. Myers, *The Foreign Policies of Herbert Hoover*, p. 53. Hereafter cited as Myers, *Hoover's Foreign Policies*. See also Jesús M. Yepes, *Le panaméricanisme au point de vue historique, juridique et politique*, pp. 154–55.

[7] Stimson and Bundy, *op. cit.*, p. 185; also Stimson, "Bases of American Foreign Policy During the Past Four Years," *Foreign Affairs*, XI (April 1933), 394. Hereafter referred to as Stimson, "Bases of American Foreign Policy."

[8] See Nerval, *Autopsy of the Monroe Doctrine*. Alfredo L. Palacios, in an open

sentment was buttressed by the thoughtless attitude of many Americans toward the doctrine, as evidenced by a senator who declared that "it was given us in Providence to state and interpret the Monroe Doctrine.[9] From previous experience, the people of Latin America had little faith in providence; they looked upon the Monroe Doctrine as a beacon of *yanqui* imperialism. An example of the extreme sensitivity of Latin pride toward the Roosevelt corollary, with its implications of inferiority and tutelage, is an episode that occurred during the closing months of the Hoover administration.

In November 1932, one of Latin America's leading newspapers, *La Prensa* of Buenos Aires, carried an editorial attacking a story written by a Japanese journalist and published in Tokyo.[10] The Japanese article referred to a conversation between Theodore Roosevelt and a Japanese nobleman, which took place shortly after the Russo-Japanese war and which centered on the idea of the Monroe Doctrine as interpreted by Roosevelt. Roosevelt was alleged to have boasted of his personal guardianship over the semicivilized peoples of Latin America, particularly those of the Caribbean region. He supposedly had suggested that Japan proclaim an Asiatic Monroe Doctrine of its own and exercise a similar guardianship over the backward Asiatic races during their transitory period. The journalist considered the Rough Rider's idea a good one, and advocated the promulgation of a Japanese Monroe Doctrine. This apparently cut deeply into sensitive Argentine pride. *La Prensa* boldly asserted that Argentinians were much more civilized and culturally further advanced than were the Japanese. The Argentine minister in Tokyo registered a protest with the Japanese government over the article, and a short time later a retraction was published. *La Prensa* praised the action of the alert foreign-service officer and declared that Argentina's diplomatic protest merited the support and emulation of other Latin-American powers.[11]

When Hoover took up the reins of government, the Monroe Doc-

letter to the youth of America, attacked the Monroe Doctrine and labeled Theodore Roosevelt a "great *condottiero*"; see *Anales de la facultad de ciencias jurídicas y sociales de la Plata,* V (1930), 818–56. In voting to join the League of Nations officially, the Argentine Chamber of Deputies refused to recognize the Monroe Doctrine and took exception to Article XXI of the covenant; see the *New York Times,* September 29, 1932.

[9] Quoted in James W. Garner, "Recrudescence of the Monroe Doctrine," *Political Science Quarterly,* XLV (June 1930), 250.

[10] *La Prensa* (Buenos Aires), November 5, 1932.

[11] *Ibid.* For a slightly different version of Roosevelt's suggestion, see the *New York Times,* August 25, 1932.

trine had become a barrier to cordial inter-American relations, and the United States was involved directly or indirectly in the internal affairs of about a half-dozen Caribbean countries.[12] In order to carry out his shift in the nation's Latin-American policy and to demonstrate his friendship for the peoples to the south, it was necessary for Hoover to remove from the Monroe Doctrine the onus of the Roosevelt corollary and, particularly, the stigma of its being used as a camouflage for American intervention. Hoover did this by adopting as his own, and issuing as a public document, a comprehensive *Memorandum on the Monroe Doctrine*, which was prepared by an eminent international lawyer and a former Undersecretary of State, J. Reuben Clark.[13]

This interpretation of the formula of 1823 was written near the end of the Coolidge administration at the request of Secretary of State Kellogg and submitted to him under the date of December 17, 1928. It was based on state papers and the pronouncements of statesmen and authorities. The study was devoted primarily to stripping Monroe's original message of its various excrescences and corollaries. It struck directly at the Roosevelt corollary, which proclaimed the principle that inasmuch as the United States would permit no European nation to intervene in the affairs of Latin-American countries, it must therefore act as an international policeman and assume the responsibility of preserving order and protecting life and property in these countries.[14] Clark denounced the use of the doctrine for such purposes, by declaring that "it is not believed that this corollary is justified by the terms of the Monroe Doctrine, however much it may be justified by the application of the doctrine of self-preservation."[15] Clark did not denounce all intervention, but mainly that which was practiced under the mantle of the Monroe Doctrine; nor did he renounce the right of unilateral interpretation of the doctrine by the United States.

The former Undersecretary of State concluded his study by reassuring the Latin-American countries that they had nothing to fear from the Monroe Doctrine, as it was not "an instrument of violence and oppression" but "a wholly effective guaranty of their freedom, independence, and territorial integrity against the imperialistic designs of Europe."[16] Originally the Clark document was not intended for

---

[12] Stimson and Bundy, *op. cit.,* p. 176.

[13] See J. Reuben Clark, *Memorandum on the Monroe Doctrine.*

[14] For Roosevelt's statement of his corollary, see his annual messages of December 6, 1904, *Congressional Record,* 58th Cong., 3d sess., p. 19, and of December 5, 1905, *ibid.,* 59th Cong., 1st sess., pp. 97–98.

[15] Clark, *op. cit.,* pp. xxiii–iv.   [16] *Ibid.,* p. xxv.

public consumption, as President Coolidge was not in accord with its principles, and for some time after it was composed it remained, without having been used, in the files of the State Department.[17] Hoover knew of its existence, and since his ideas were in line with those expressed by the memorandum, he adopted it when he became President as a means of implementing his good-neighbor policy.[18] In the early part of 1930 he had it published as a public document, and thereby indicated to the governments of Latin America that his administration would be guided to a large extent by its principles—though by this time Hoover had gone much further than the document suggested.[19] He had committed himself to a policy of nonintervention, regardless of the form under which it might be practiced.

In the last few days of the Coolidge administration, and prior to the publication of the Clark study, Secretary of State Kellogg prepared a concise "official statement of and commentary upon the Monroe Doctrine" that was sent confidentially to all of the United States diplomatic missions in Latin America.[20] The American diplomatic officials were instructed to hold the commentary until they were notified by the Secretary of State to communicate it to the ministers of foreign affairs in the various countries. Kellogg's statement was a short historical study of the origin and purpose of the Monroe Doctrine and in content was similar to the Clark memorandum. It was prepared with the intention of clearing away misunderstandings in reference to the Monroe Doctrine, and it also reassured the southern peoples that they need not fear intervention under the doctrine's guise. Kellogg reiterated that the Monroe Doctrine was directed solely against European powers who might attempt to interfere in the affairs of the Western Hemisphere. He also made it clear that in so far as the Latin-American nations in general were concerned, Monroe's fiat did not presume to protect these countries against European action, provided such action did not take the form of oppressing or controlling them in any manner.[21]

In a letter to Secretary Stimson, several months after the promulgation of the Clark interpretation, Kellogg suggested that his note be delivered to the various Latin-American countries, and that it then be published.[22] Stimson immediately forwarded his predecessor's sug-

---

[17] Mr. Hoover's statement in personal interview, August 5, 1947.   [18] *Ibid.*
[19] See *New York Times,* June 24, 1930; also editorial, *ibid.,* June 25, 1930.
[20] For the complete text of the document, see *Foreign Relations, 1929,* I, 698–719.
[21] See *ibid.,* pp. 698–719.   [22] *Ibid.,* p. 719.

gestion to Hoover, who replied that he considered it unwise to put it out at that time, as it "would provoke a great deal of debate and may cause embarrassment in other matters."[23] When the Clark memorandum was finally published, the pressure of governmental business, particularly that of the London Naval Conference, had delayed the delivery of the Kellogg note.[24] In the last two years of the administration the pressure increased so that the note apparently was never delivered, even though it represented the viewpoint of the administration.

The publication of the Clark document met with a favorable reception in general, both at home and abroad. The idea that the Monroe Doctrine was to be used "for the defense rather than the domination of Latin America" aided considerably in dispelling fear of the "colossus of the north" harbored by many of the southern nations. The reaction of press opinion in the United States was favorable. This was indicated by two separate analyses of the editorial comment concerning the Clark memorandum in the newspapers of the United States.[25] Editorial comment was overwhelmingly friendly to the pronouncement, but revealed a wide variance in the interpretation of it.

A survey of a portion of the Latin-American press showed general approval of the document, but it also revealed some unfriendly critics.[26] A section of the Mexican press attacked the memorandum and indicated a greater confidence in Mexico's Estrada Doctrine. *La Crítica* of Argentina was quoted as proclaiming that the Monroe Doctrine had wholly outlived its usefulness, despite Clark's words. However, most newspapers considered the document as having cleared the atmosphere. They looked upon it as a reflection of Hoover's opinion, and as an indication of a new orientation in the Latin-American policy of the United States.

Keeping in line with its good-neighbor policy, the Hoover administration went beyond the implications of Clark's words. It sought to reassure the peoples of the south that the sting had been completely

[23] Hoover Papers, Stimson to Hoover, June 25, 1930, and Hoover to Stimson, June 26, 1930.

[24] See the *New York Times,* June 24, 1930.

[25] Among the miscellaneous papers in the Hoover Archives is an editorial analysis which seems to bear this out; it is a survey of thirty-four papers, by unknown authors, dated July 11, 1930. Another confidential analysis, prepared by the Division of Historical Policy Research of the State Department, surveying one hundred ten papers, shows the same trend.

[26] Summaries of various Latin-American newspaper comments prepared by the Division of Historical Policy Research of the Department of State showed this.

removed from the Monroe Doctrine. Secretary of State Stimson, in a public address on inter-American relations shortly after the promulgation of Clark's thesis, interpreted the Monroe Doctrine in Clark's terms and reiterated his principle that "the Monroe Doctrine was a declaration of the United States versus Europe—not of the United States versus Latin America." He continued by declaring that "in taking this position in the Western Hemisphere, our policy has coincided with the basic conception of international law, namely, the equal rights of each nation in the family of nations."[27]

A sampling of Latin-American press comment, referring to Stimson's statement of policy, indicated a mixed, though on the whole favorable, reaction.[28] *La Nación* of Buenos Aires was critical and was quoted as stressing the idea that "the formula of 1823 cannot be fitted to life in 1930." *La Prensa* of the same city noted that the departure of Hoover from the policies of his predecessors was too apparent for Stimson's speech not to assume the character of an important public declaration of opinions and purposes.

The Department of State continued placating the fears of the sensitive American republics by often assuring them that the Monroe Doctrine was to be used only for their protection, not their destruction. Undersecretary of State William R. Castle, Jr., stressed this principle a year later by declaring that "the Monroe Doctrine confers no superior position on the United States."[29] He made his point clear to all when he exclaimed that "in the protection of American interests in Latin-American countries, the Monroe Doctrine has no more place than in the protection of those interests in the Orient."[30] At the same time another official denied that the Monroe thesis implied tutelage.[31] In all these ways it was brought home to the peoples of Latin America that the Hoover policy was one of peace and nonintervention.

[27] Henry L. Stimson, *The United States and the Other American Republics,* p. 2. This speech was delivered before the Council on Foreign Relations of New York on February 6, 1931.

[28] This was shown in the excerpts from various Latin-American newspapers, located in the files of the Columbus Memorial Library of the Pan American Union in Washington, D.C.

[29] Department of State Press Releases, No. 92 (July 4, 1931), p. 31. This address, entitled "Aspects of the Monroe Doctrine," explains clearly the administration's view of the doctrine.

[30] *Ibid.*

[31] Walter C. Thurston, "Relations With Our Latin American Neighbors," *Annals of the American Academy of Political and Social Science,* CLVI (July 1931), 121; Thurston was at this time chief of the Latin-American Division in the Department of State.

CHAPTER VI

RECOGNITION POLICIES

"We certainly cannot deny to other nations that principle whereon our government is founded, that every nation has a right to govern itself internally under what forms it pleases, and to change these forms at its own will; and externally to transact business with other nations through whatever organ it chooses, whether that be a King, Convention, Assembly, Committee, President, or whatever it be."
> —THOMAS JEFFERSON, 1792

Recognition or nonrecognition of new, revolutionary Latin-American governments has always been a powerful political weapon in the hands of the President of the United States. Granting recognition to one faction and not to another has often been a form of intervention in Latin-American affairs as potent as a landing force of Marines.[1] As recognition is a political act of the chief executive, in no way circumscribed by Congress or the courts, the use made of this power reflects strongly upon the foreign policy of an administration.[2] At times the inadvertent exercise of the recognition prerogative has led to embarrassing diplomatic difficulties, and even to long-smoldering animosities in inter-American relations.[3]

In its use of the recognition power as applied to the nations of Latin America, the Hoover administration followed two distinct and separate policies. One was a specific policy that was employed only in relation to the five Central American republics of Costa Rica, Guatemala, Honduras, Nicaragua, and El Salvador. This can properly be called the special recognition policy. The administration applied the other well-defined policy to the South American nations and all other Latin-American republics not encompassed in the special policy. It can be referred to as the general recognition policy.[4]

---

[1] See Stimson and Bundy, *On Active Service*, p. 178; Nerval, *Autopsy of the Monroe Doctrine*, pp. 282–84.

[2] See Williams, "Recognition," pp. 71–75; also Green H. Hackworth, *Digest of International Law*, I, 161–66.

[3] See Stimson and Bundy, *op. cit.*, pp. 177–78; Nerval, *op. cit.*, pp. 283–84.

[4] Myers, *Hoover's Foreign Policies*, p. 45; Department of State, "Review of Questions," I, 1.

The day after his inauguration, Hoover was informed by the out-going Secretary of State, Frank B. Kellogg, of the then prevailing recognition policy, which was applicable to all Latin-American repub-lics. According to this policy, the United States granted recognition only to those governments that came to power through lawful means, and it would not recognize any regime that gained control of a country through a coup d'état, revolution, or other unconstitutional means.[5] This was the formula first tried by President Wilson in 1913 and adopted by succeeding administrations, until abandoned by Hoover in favor of the traditional recognition policy of the United States, enun-ciated by Thomas Jefferson and generally followed since his day.[6] Both Hoover and his Secretary of State were opposed to the Wilson theory of recognition, on the grounds that it was ineffectual in prac-tice even if it might be theoretically justifiable.[7] Because of the great size and power of the United States—in comparison to the southern countries—and the extent to which its lead was followed by other powers of the world, the nonrecognition principle was in effect a form of intervention. As Hoover had definitely turned his back on inter-vention, the recognition policy had to be changed.

The problem of recognition became of pressing importance in the second half of 1930, when a wave of revolutions, propelled by political discontent resulting from the world economic depression, swept over Latin America.[8] Throughout this turbulent period the Hoover ad-ministration adhered steadily to its general policy of recognizing each revolutionary government as soon as it had actual control of the country and it became evident that there was no effective resistance to its rule, provided it indicated its intention of fulfilling its international obligations.[9] This threefold criterion for granting recognition was succinctly set forth by Stimson in a statement of September 17, 1930, when he announced that he had instructed the American diplomatic missions in Argentina, Bolivia, and Peru "to resume normal diplo-

[5] Hoover Papers, Kellogg to Hoover, March 5, 1929; see also Myers, *Hoover's Foreign Policies*, p. 45.

[6] For Jefferson's point of view, see Jefferson to Pinckney, December 30, 1792, in Andrew A. Lipscomb, ed., *The Writings of Thomas Jefferson*, IX, 7–8; see also statement by Green H. Hackworth in Department of State Press Releases, No. 82 (April 25, 1931), pp. 353–54.

[7] See Stimson and Bundy, *op. cit.*, p. 178.

[8] See Lippman and Scroggs, eds., *The United States in World Affairs, 1931*, p. 44; Toynbee, *International Affairs, 1930*, p. 366; Stimson and Bundy, *op. cit.*, p. 177.

[9] Department of State, "Review of Questions," Part I, p. 1; Stimson and Bundy, *op. cit.*, p. 177.

matic relations" with the provisional government in each of these countries.[10] Unquestionably, the governments of these countries had arisen from revolutions in which the legally constituted authorities had been overthrown. In addition to the other recognition requirements, Stimson anticipated that in due course the new regimes would sponsor elections to "regularize their status."

Besides stating the grounds for the general policy, Stimson gave the administration's reasons for abandoning Wilson's policy, and emphasized that "in acting toward these three Governments" in the matter of recognition, "we are following the regular rules of international law, and the regular policy which has characterized this country ever since the first Secretary of State announced it—Mr. Jefferson in the Administration of President Washington."[11] Ascertainable public reaction to Stimson's pronouncement and to the administration's general recognition policy was definitely favorable. Press comment in the United States, though varied in its interpretation of the policy, indicated a highly pleased response.[12]

The general policy was then quickly put to use in subsequent cases, such as that of Brazil. After their successful revolution of October 1930, the new provisional authorities of Brazil promptly requested recognition from the United States in a note which asserted a desire to respect national obligations contracted abroad as well as treaties and other international obligations.[13] The Hoover administration then replied that it was ready to continue the same friendly relations with the new government of Brazil as maintained with its predecessors.[14] Immediate recognition was also given to the new, provisional junta of Peru that came into power in May 1931 after a tumultuous uprising.[15]

In other instances, before the Department of State acknowledged that formal recognition was unnecessary because constitutional forms had been observed in the change of government, it examined the situation closely on the basis of the conditions enunciated by Stimson.[16]

---

[10] For the full text, see *Foreign Relations, 1930*, I, 387–89; also *New York Times*, September 18, 1930.

[11] *Ibid.* The administration also felt that prompt recognition would aid these governments in their struggle against the economic depression; see Stimson, "Bases of American Foreign Policy," p. 395.

[12] An editorial analysis of one hundred thirteen American newspapers, found among the miscellaneous papers in the Hoover Archives and dated September 29, 1930, bears this out.   [13] *Foreign Relations, 1930*, I, 445.   [14] *Ibid.*, p. 451.

[15] See Stimson to Dearing, *Foreign Relations, 1931*, II, 921.

[16] Department of State, "Review of Questions," I, 2; *Foreign Relations, 1931*, II, 892–902.

This procedure was used in relation to Panama, following the quick revolution of January 2, 1931. Recognition given to the previous regime by Washington was automatically extended to the new government.[17]

The problem of Chile was complicated by the sudden coming into power in June 1932 of a military junta headed by Carlos Dávila, which advocated and tried to carry out socialistic policies.[18] The Hoover administration therefore placed great stress on obtaining satisfactory assurances as to the willingness of this regime to fulfill its international obligations. When a series of kaleidoscopic governmental changes took place under Dávila's leadership and it looked as if a socialistic constitution might be adopted, the Department of State announced an additional twofold principle for the junta's recognition. It maintained "that there should be no discrimination in the protection which must be accorded to the nationals of other countries and their property," and then emphasized that both "must be accorded a degree of protection at least as high as that given to natives of the country, and secondly that this standard of protection must not fall below the minimum standard set by international law and practice."[19] Aside from protecting American rights, it was not the policy of the Hoover government to associate recognition with a particular type of government or political institution in any Latin-American country. However, the recognition of the Dávila regime never did take place, since it was overthrown in September of the same year and was succeeded by another, less radical, provisional administration.[20]

The reversion to the traditional policy of recognition was limited to those ordinary cases where international practice was not affected or controlled by pre-existing treaty.[21] In five of the six Central American states, an entirely different situation faced the United States from that normally covered by international law and practice. In this area, the Hoover administration was guided by the same policy that was followed by preceding American governments since 1907. This special recognition procedure was first adopted in a treaty in 1907 and was reiterated in the General Treaty of Peace and Amity of February

---

[17] *Ibid.*, pp. 903–4.

[18] Department of State, "Review of Questions," Part I, p. 2; see also *New York Times,* June 5 and 6, 1932.

[19] Department of State, "Review of Questions," Part I, pp. 2–3.

[20] *Ibid.*, p. 4; *New York Times*, September 14, 1932.

[21] See Stimson's speech of September 17, 1930, in *Foreign Relations, 1930,* I, 387–89.

1923, enacted by the five Central American republics in Washington, D.C. This treaty provided that governments which came into power in any of the five signatory republics through revolution, coup d'état, or other illegal means used against a recognized legal government, should not be recognized "so long as the freely elected representatives of the people thereof have not constitutionally reorganized the country."[22] The treaty also contained specified restrictions, prohibiting the accession to office, as head of the state, of any person who had previously held certain designated offices.[23]

The purpose of the treaty was to discourage the more turbulent elements of these republics from resorting to periodic rebellions and military uprisings. Although fraught with "possible difficulties and dangers of application," and despite the fact that the United States was not a signatory of the 1923 treaty, the provisions for recognition were interpreted by Secretary of State Hughes as likewise applying to United States relations with the signatory powers.[24] This special recognition policy was used on two occasions during the Hoover administration, once applied to Guatemala and the other time to El Salvador.

In Guatemala, a series of governmental changes was started when President Lázaro Chacón became seriously ill at the end of 1930 and temporarily retired to receive treatment in New Orleans. He died there in April 1931.[25] Upon Chacón's retirement, the second presidential designate, Señor Baudilio Palma, succeeded him and was promptly recognized by the United States.[26] But within a few days, his government was overturned by a military coup d'état, and the leader of the revolt, General Manuel Orellana, was declared provisional president by the legislature. The Washington government then announced that as Orellana had violated the Central American treaty of 1923, he would not be recognized; nor was his government recognized by the other republics of Central America.[27] This compelled Orellana to resign in favor of José María Reina Andrade, who, after the resignation of the incapacitated Chacón, was constitutionally

[22] For the text of the treaty and proceedings of the meeting in Spanish and English, see Department of State, *Conference on Central American Affairs.*

[23] Article II specified the recognition practice; see *ibid.*, pp. 288–89.

[24] See the statement by Hughes in *Foreign Relations, 1923,* II, 432–34. Stimson believed this special policy had been "productive of very great good," by reducing the incidence of bloodshed in Central America; see Stimson and Bundy, *op. cit.,* p. 179.

[25] *Foreign Relations, 1930,* III, 172; Jones, *Guatemala Past and Present,* p. 69.

[26] *Foreign Relations, 1930,* III, 175.

[27] *Ibid.,* pp. 176–83.

designated provisional president by the Guatemalan Congress at the beginning of January 1931. The United States and the other four Central American republics immediately recognized his government.[28] He promptly called for a new election, in which Jorge Ubico was chosen constitutional president of Guatemala.

The Hoover administration ran into complications in applying the special recognition policy to El Salvador. The problem of recognition came up when a successful military revolt broke out in the first days of December 1931, which forced the constitutional president, Arturo Araujo, to flee the country.[29] Following the departure of Araujo, Vice-President General Maximiliano Hernández Martínez, who had also been minister of war, declared himself president of the republic. After sending Jefferson Caffery on a special mission in the middle of December to inquire into the situation in El Salvador, the Department of State declared that the *de facto* regime of Martínez was barred from recognition under the terms of Article II of the 1923 treaty.[30] The reason behind this nonrecognition was that Martínez was apparently implicated in the plot that caused the downfall of Araujo, thereby violating provisions of the treaty.[31] So strong was the indication of Martínez' participation that the minister of foreign affairs of Honduras labeled the episode an "abominable treason."[32] On January 8, 1932, the United States minister to El Salvador was recalled. He departed two days later, leaving the legation in the hands of the chargé d'affaires ad interim.

Despite the action of the United States, which was usually sufficient to cause any Central American government to topple, Martínez was able to remain in power. He played for, and succeeded in obtaining, the sympathy and support of his people, and in the latter part of January he smashed an uprising supposedly engineered by Communists. As a consequence, his position became considerably stronger, and in February he was declared constitutional president of the republic by the legislative assembly. In time, the stand maintained by Martínez gained him the sympathetic support of Costa Rica, which urged the other signatories of the 1923 Washington agreements to join her in denouncing these onerous treaties.[33]

[28] See *ibid., 1931,* II, 393–400.

[29] See *ibid.,* pp. 169 ff.; also the *New York Times,* December 4 and 5, 1931.

[30] See *Foreign Relations, 1931,* II, 201–12; also the *New York Times,* December 6, 8, and 18, 1931.

[31] Department of State, "Review of Questions," Part I, pp. 14–15.

[32] *Ibid.,* pp. 13–14.   [33] *Ibid.,* pp. 30–34.

Facing a growing sentiment in favor of recognition, the State Department decided to clarify its position. In November 1932, it sent a long note to the American legation in Guatemala, stating that although the United States was not a signatory of the 1923 treaty, it considered that the advantages derived by Central America from the treaty warranted making an exception to its traditional practice of recognizing new governments. The note continued that if the treaty were abrogated, the United States "would resume its freedom of action and would henceforth judge each case upon its merits as it arose."[34] The majority of the Central American states were in favor of upholding the established policy, but in December 1932 Costa Rica and El Salvador issued decrees denouncing the General Treaty of Peace and Amity of 1923; the denunciation to be effective on January 1, 1934, in conformity with Article XVIII of the treaty.[35]

Although they later joined in denouncing the treaty, at that time Nicaragua, Honduras, and Guatemala indicated a desire to keep the treaty in effect. This was in accordance with Article XVIII, which provided that the treaty should remain in force as long as at least three of the ratifying powers did not denounce it.[36] Approximately a year after Hoover went out of office, Costa Rica recognized the Martínez government. The other republics soon followed her lead, as did the new administration in the United States.[37] Thus came to an end the special recognition policy.

[34] Department of State, "Review of Questions," Part I, pp. 34–35.

[35] Ibid., p. 39; for the text of Article XVIII, see Department of State, Conference on Central American Affairs, p. 294.

[36] Department of State, "Review of Questions," Part I, p. 40; New York Times, January 27, 1934. See also William L. Neumann, Jr., Recognition of Governments in the Americas, p. 24.

[37] See New York Times, January 4 and 27, 1934; Neumann, op. cit., p. 24. Earlier, Great Britain and a number of European and Asiatic powers had recognized the Martínez government.

CHAPTER VII

RENUNCIATION OF INTERVENTION AND DOLLAR DIPLOMACY

"Perhaps diplomatic intervention has sometimes been unwise, even unfair. One hears of 'dollar diplomacy.' If this ever existed it has, thank God, gone the way of all bad policies."
—UNDERSECRETARY OF STATE WILLIAM R. CASTLE, 1931

Long before he became President, Hoover was known to be opposed to United States intervention in Latin America. As early as 1922, when he was Secretary of Commerce, it was intimated that he was in favor of withdrawing the Marines from Haiti and Santo Domingo. On his good-will tour one of the most important contributions he made was to stress that intervention would not be the policy of the United States in the future. In his address delivered at Guayaquil, Ecuador, he expressed his attitude toward intervention with the concise statement that "true democracy is not and cannot be imperialistic. The brotherhood of this faith is the guarantee of good will."[1]

Early in the second month of his administration, Hoover chose the occasion of a Gridiron Club dinner to emphasize his aversion to dollar diplomacy and to intervention in the internal affairs of Latin-American countries. After expressing his appreciation for the courtesy and good will shown him on his visit to Latin America, he declared:

And in this connection of the relations of great and little nations may I mention one sinister notion, fear of which I detect in some sections of the press, as to policies of the United States bearing basically upon our relationships with our Latin-American Neighbors? That is, fear of an era of the mistakenly called dollar diplomacy. The implications that have been colored by that expression are not a part of my conception of international relations. I can say at once that it never has been and ought not to be the policy of the United States to intervene by force to secure or maintain contracts between our citizens and foreign States or their citizens. Confidence in that attitude is the only basis upon which the economic co-operation of our citizens can be welcomed

---

[1] *Hoover's Latin-American Addresses*, p. 16.

59

abroad. It is the only basis that prevents cupidity encroaching upon the weakness of nations—but, far more than this, it is the true expression of the moral rectitude of the United States.[2]

This pronouncement constituted a pointed intimation that the attitude of the giant northern republic toward its Latin neighbors was changing. Not only was the new President against political and military intervention in the internal affairs of the Latin-American countries, but he was also strongly opposed to intervention for the purpose of protecting private American investments.

How much the Latin-American policy of the United States had changed in the four years of the Hoover regime is shown by the action of the administration during its last days. At the meeting of the governing board of the Pan American Union, on January 4, 1933, Assistant Secretary of State Francis White, representing Stimson, agreed without exception to Argentina's proposition to place on the agenda of the forthcoming Pan-American conference at Montevideo the draft of an antiwar treaty prepared by its Foreign Minister, Dr. Carlos Saavedra Lamas. The proposed antiwar objectives were already covered by the Kellogg-Briand peace pact; the real essence of the Argentine plan was the rejection of intervention in any form. This was in actuality a maneuver to throw the subject of intervention into the arena of debate at Montevideo and there, in the presence of the assembled delegates, spearhead an attack against the past policies of the United States. The attitude of the Washington government was significant, because it revealed that Hoover and Stimson were not only opposed to the practice of intervention but were even ready to relinquish the legal "right" of intervention.[3] They were thus prepared to go beyond the limits of international law in their renunciation of intervention. The Latin-American policy of the nation had traveled far on the road to good-neighborliness since the Havana conference of 1928, where Hughes had ably defended the legal "right" of intervention.

Probably the most striking phase of the Latin-American policy of the Hoover administration was "its deliberate pursuit of nonintervention in the sensitive Central American and Caribbean area."[4] An

[2] The address was delivered April 13, 1929, in Washington, D.C.; for the full text, see Myers, ed., *Hoover Papers*, I, 27–31.

[3] See Samuel F. Bemis, *The Latin American Policy of the United States*, pp. 268–69. Later President Roosevelt and Secretary of State Hull also accepted the Argentine program without objections.

[4] Stimson and Bundy, *On Active Service*, p. 182.

example of this was Hoover's outright avoidance of intervention at the outbreak of a seven-hour revolution in the Isthmian republic of Panama. This uprising swept the administration of President Florencio Harmodio Arosemena from power in the early morning hours of January 2, 1931.[5] The United States carefully refrained from interfering in any way in the progress of the revolt, although at least one American citizen was killed.[6] The attitude of the Hoover administration was noteworthy, as the preceding administration had indicated that the people of Panama would not be allowed any revolutionary privileges.[7] Thus, the first revolution in the tiny republic of Panama was made possible by a definite reversal of policy by the United States. That a Washington government would allow a revolution to take place near its vital canal and not exercise treaty rights to intervene was a significant break with the past.[8] The administration maintained its policy of restraint. It did not interfere in Panamanian affairs when in May 1931 a clash between United States military police and Panama police in Colón aroused hostile feelings between the two countries.[9]

The same policy of restraint was exercised by the Hoover administration when an insurrection broke out in another Central American republic. In April 1931, the Indian general and professional revolutionist, Gregorio Ferrera, who had a large following among the Indian workers of the American-owned fruit plantations, led a revolt against the existing government of Honduras. During the course of hostilities, American property, primarily that of the United Fruit Company, was attacked and looted, and the lives of American citizens were endangered.[10] In consequence, the United States sent several warships to Honduran waters, confining their activities, however, "to

[5] See *Foreign Relations, 1931,* II, 890–93 and 894–902, which gives a historical account of the revolution; *New York Times,* January 3 to 8, 1931; also William David McCain, *The United States and the Republic of Panama,* pp. 90–91.

[6] *New York Times,* January 3, 7, and 8, 1931; McCain, *op. cit.,* p. 90. The Panamanian government requested that the United States send troops into the country. This appeal was categorically refused; see *Foreign Relations, 1931,* II, 890–91.

[7] McCain, *op. cit.,* p. 90. See Kellogg's statement of July 27, 1928, in *Foreign Relations, 1928,* III, 678.

[8] See Raymond L. Buell, "Changes in Our Latin American Policy," *Annals of the American Academy of Political and Social Science,* CLVI (July 1931), 131–32; also Allan Nevins, "President Hoover's Record," *Current History,* XXXVI (July 1932), 392.

[9] See *New York Times,* May 11, 1931; *ibid.,* August 19, 1931.

[10] *Foreign Relations, 1931,* II, 555–82; Department of State, "Review of Questions," Part I, p. 80; *New York Times,* April 20 to 23, 1931.

making provision for the safety of American lives and property in the coast towns."[11] Except for evacuation by these warships of several hundred Americans employed by the American fruit companies, there was no intervention by the United States. Secretary Stimson stressed the American policy of nonintervention by maintaining that the revolutionary movement was an internal matter, to be handled solely by the Honduran government, and that the United States would not participate in any way. This pronouncement was later published by the Honduran press and was highly praised.[12] Several diplomatic incidents occurred during the course of the uprising, which involved the United States; but they had no serious consequences. With the death of Ferrera, early in June 1931, the revolt automatically collapsed, and the United States recalled its warships.[13]

After the 1932 elections in Honduras, another rebellion broke out. Despite the repeated appeals for aid from the Honduran government, and the evident aid given the insurgents by El Salvador, the United States scrupulously maintained its policy of noninterference. By the end of December, the Honduran government had decisively defeated the rebel forces and reasserted its authority.[14]

In line with the administration's policy of respecting the independence and integrity of all nations of the American continent, Secretary of State Stimson delivered a nationwide broadcast on May 9, 1931, in which he explained to the American people the purpose of the government's Latin-American policy.[15] He characterized certain difficulties and misunderstandings in Latin-American–United States relations as "sore spots," and stated that they "have damaged our good name, our credit, and our trade far beyond the apprehension of our own people. The State Department is addressing itself seriously and successfully toward the removal of these sore spots." He then enumerated some of the ways in which the United States had sought "to eradicate the sore spots of Latin-American diplomacy," and added that the press comments throughout the Western continent "have indicated that the effort has not been unsuccessful."[16]

[11] Department of State, "Review of Questions," Part I, pp. 30–31; also Department of State Press Releases, No. 82 (April 25, 1931), p. 312.

[12] Department of State, "Review of Questions," Part I, p. 83.

[13] Ibid., p. 86; Foreign Relations, 1931, II, 581–82.

[14] Department of State, "Review of Questions," Part I, p. 92; New York Times, December 25 and 31, 1932.

[15] For the complete text of the speech, see Department of State Press Releases, No. 84 (May 9, 1931), pp. 386–92; also the United States Daily, May 10, 1931.

[16] Department of State Press Releases, No. 84 (May 9, 1931), pp. 390–91.

Stimson served notice that intervention was being abandoned, and that the Hoover administration was adhering to the principle, enunciated by Elihu Root when he was Secretary of State, that the Army and Navy would not be used to collect debts from weaker powers. Stimson stressed the intention that the people of Latin America should be left alone to manage their own affairs. He spoke of Pan-American solidarity, of trying to promote a policy of good will and mutual trust, and maintained that good relations with Latin America "constitute one of the cardinal tenets of our foreign policy." He concluded the address by tying together the Latin-American and general foreign policies of the administration and emphasizing the good-neighbor approach in the Western Hemisphere.[17] Public reaction to Stimson's words was varied but generally favorable throughout the United States.[18]

Hoover's reluctance to use military intervention in Panama, Honduras, and El Salvador, and his steps toward the liquidation of imperialism in Nicaragua and Haiti were a vital part of his Pan-American program. This was aimed at the removal of the suspicion with which Latin America had viewed United States motives in inter-American relations. In another Gridiron Club speech in April 1930, the President underscored this objective of his Latin-American policy by warning that "there began to pervade the world a jealousy, a suspicion, and an ill will toward the United States, such as never before existed in peace history. Therefore, it became the first duty of the American officials responsible for the foreign policies of the Government to realign this sentiment and this public opinion in the world back to the true actualities of American aspirations."[19] He referred to the fear with which many Latin-American countries viewed United States economic expansion; an expansion that some characterized as a species of national arrogance. He asserted that "a large part of the world had come to believe that they were in the presence of the birth of a new imperial power intent upon dominating the destinies and freedom of other peoples." He repudiated this viewpoint, which he labeled a misconception, and then enumerated the various measures taken by his administration to supplant the patent animosity with good will and amity. He concluded by declaring that the United States

---

[17] *Ibid.*, pp. 389–92.

[18] This was indicated by an editorial analysis found among the miscellaneous presidential papers in the Hoover Archives, dated May 13, 1931, the authorship of which is unknown.

[19] For the complete text, see Myers, ed., *Hoover Papers*, I, 267–72.

was aiming for progress "by the creation of good will and human advancement and not by exploitation."

The Hoover administration's financial policy toward Latin America was based on the abandonment of "dollar diplomacy." It had often made clear its intention to enforce no private concessions entered into by Americans and Latin-American governments, and to collect no debts by military threats.[20] The Washington government took the stand that American citizens should not seek official support in their private transactions in Latin America, unless their claims were reasonable in themselves and they sought redress after exhausting the usual legal facilities of the country in which they had a grievance. If such a procedure were followed, then the United States required only that its nationals be accorded treatment equal to that given to other foreigners, and that it not fall below the minimum standard set by international practice.[21]

This policy was carried still further when, in April 1931, Nicaraguan insurgents under General Sandino attacked and killed about nine Americans near the town of Puerto Cabezas on the east coast of Nicaragua.[22] Upon learning of the attack, the State Department at once had war vessels ordered to the scene of action. Then, on April 16, 1931, Secretary Stimson sent a telegram to the American foreign-service officials in Nicaragua, announcing a new protection policy to be followed by the Hoover administration.[23] He indicated that American citizens who carried on business in Latin America did so at their own risk, and that they could not expect to be protected by United States forces, even though their lives as well as their property might be in danger. This was a complete reversal of President Coolidge's position that Americans and their property were to be protected by the government "wherever they may be."[24]

Stimson made known that the "government cannot undertake general protection of Americans throughout that country with American forces."[25] To have assumed such protection would have led the government into difficulties and commitments which Stimson made clear the government did not propose to undertake. He then laid

[20] See Department of State Press Releases, No. 84 (May 9, 1931), p. 392.

[21] Department of State, "Review of Questions," Part I, p. 3.

[22] Foreign Relations, 1931, II, 805; see also the New York Times, April 15 and 16, 1931.

[23] For the text, see Foreign Relations, 1931, II, 808.

[24] See Coolidge's speech, defending his administration's foreign policy in the New York Times, April 26, 1927.   [25] Foreign Relations, 1931, II, 808.

down the policy that Americans who did not feel secure in the interior should withdraw from the country or go to the coast towns where the United States government would give them protection or evacuate them.

Although this was an innovation in Latin-American relations, the principle of extending protection to American citizens only in coastal areas was not new in United States foreign affairs.[26] This policy was adopted by the State Department in 1927 in connection with disorders in China. But it was strikingly important in Central America because, if the old policy had been followed, active intervention by American forces would have been almost certain.

Public reaction to Stimson's declaration was instantaneous, and the press generally favored it, although a large section expressed hostility to the new policy.[27] Answering the vociferous attacks of the newspapers which did not favor the policy, particularly the Hearst chain, Stimson amplified and justified it in a formal statement on April 18, 1931.[28] He conveyed the opinion that the outbreak was "a problem with which the sovereign Government of Nicaragua is primarily concerned, and a problem which it is primarily the right and duty of that Government to solve." Stimson then went on to assert that there had been "no change in the determination of the American Government not to send American troops into the interior."[29] In this he was vigorously supported by President Hoover.[30]

This same policy of coastal protection only was extended to American citizens in Honduras during the April 1931 rebellion there.[31] At home and abroad, the policy was widely interpreted as a marked change in the attitude of the United States toward Central America, and was heralded as additional evidence of a nonintervention policy in the vital Caribbean area.[32]

[26] See *Foreign Relations, 1927,* II, 44 ff.; also the *New York Times,* April 26, 1931.

[27] This was indicated by a survey of seventy-six leading newspapers, made by the Foreign Policy Association; see Raymond L. Buell, "The United States and Central American Stability," *Foreign Policy Reports,* VII (July 8, 1931), p. 161; also Stimson and Bundy, *op. cit.,* pp. 181–82.

[28] For the text of this statement, see *Foreign Relations, 1931,* II, 814–16.

[29] *Ibid.* Stimson considered the Americans in Nicaragua "a pampered lot of people"; see Stimson and Bundy, *op. cit.,* p. 182.

[30] For the position taken by the President, see the *New York Times,* April 16, 1931.

[31] *Foreign Relations, 1931,* II, 571; Department of State Press Releases, No. 82 (April 25, 1931), p. 312.

[32] Buell, "The United States and Central American Stability," p. 161; see also Stimson and Bundy, *op. cit.,* p. 182.

CHAPTER VIII

DEPRESSION DIPLOMACY

". . . . the State Department should not become an insurance agency and give Americans abroad guarantees that they do not have at home." —SECRETARY OF STATE STIMSON, 1931

Hoover's Latin-American financial policy had as its background a world-wide economic crisis that struck the United States with a stock-market crash on October 29, 1929—only eight months after he had taken office. The distress of debtor nations was universal, and the depression hit Latin America with a shattering impact. As compared to other sections of the world, the foreign trade of the southern republics was almost wiped out of existence by the financial crisis.[1]

The reasons for this were many, some more decisive than others. The Latin-American countries were producers of raw materials, and deflation was especially disastrous for them. To meet debt charges and to pay for purchases abroad, most Latin-American republics were dependent on the export of one or two basic commodities, and were thus more vulnerable to economic adversities than were other countries with a more diversified output. They were almost all debtor countries. A large part of their budgets was devoted to service on their foreign debts; the burden of their contractual obligations increased greatly with the decline in value of their products. In some cases they had borrowed to excess, and the loans were not always expended for productive purposes. The economic difficulties of the Latin-American states during the depression were of special significance to inter-American relations, because of large United States investments in those countries.[2] By the beginning of the Hoover regime, more capital had been invested in Latin America by citizens of the United States than in all of Europe.[3]

[1] See Willy Feuerlein and Elizabeth Hannan, *Dollars in Latin America,* pp. 18–19; also Lippmann and Scroggs, eds., *The United States in World Affairs, 1931,* pp. 43–44.

[2] Department of State, "Review of Questions," Part III, pp. 1–3; see also Feuerlein and Hannan, *op. cit.,* pp. 13–14; Lippmann and Scroggs, eds., *op. cit.,* p. 50.

[3] *Ibid.;* also William O. Scroggs, "The American Investments in Latin America," *Foreign Affairs,* X (April 1932), 502.

This deluge of investment had its greatest impact in the period preceding and during World War I.[4] After the war, American investments continued in government bonds, railways, public utilities, packing companies, oil companies, mining operations, fruit companies, sugar industries, and numerous other undertakings, but the ratio of investment changed.[5] In the first two years of Hoover's administration the previous economic pattern persisted, and the economic development of the Latin-American countries continued apace. But in the last two years of his term in office, investments in Latin America fell off in comparison to investments in Europe, owing largely to the instability of Latin-American governments and the paralyzing effect of the depression. As a result, United States investments in Latin America by the beginning of 1932 were just slightly higher than the stake in Europe.[6]

Because of the severity of the economic depression in the southern lands, the Hoover administration's Latin-American relations were complicated by a maze of financial and economic difficulties.[7] There were numerous defaults by South American governments, states, or municipalities on bonds held by North American investors.[8] As the tempo of the world-wide economic crisis increased, the defaults assumed increasingly serious proportions. This failure of the South American countries to meet their financial obligations became the basis of considerable ill will between the people of the United States and those of the southern republics.[9] The Latin-American governments found that the depression had dried up the sources of their loans in the United States, and they were bewildered by the changed situation. North Americans wanted the money that they had loaned in good faith, while South Americans felt that, because of their prostrate condition brought about by the depression, they should be aided and not pressed by their wealthy northern neighbor. No creditor is popular in the eyes of the debtor; so it was in Hispanic America.

[4] For statistics and figures, see Max Winkler and W. W. Cumberland, "Investments and National Policy of the United States in Latin America," *American Economic Review*, XXII (March 1932) supplement, 144–84.

[5] *Ibid.;* also Department of State, "Review of Questions," Part III, pp. 1–3.

[6] Winkler and Cumberland, *op. cit.,* p. 145; Lippmann and Scroggs, eds., *op. cit.,* p. 50.

[7] Department of State, "Review of Questions," Part III, p. 1.

[8] *Ibid.,* p. 2; *Congressional Record,* 72d Cong., 1st sess., p. 6057. For default cases, see Max Winkler and Maxwell Stewart, "Recent Defaults of Government Loans," *Foreign Policy Reports,* VII (January 6, 1932), 395–97.

[9] Isaac F. Marcosson, "New Americas," *Saturday Evening Post,* CCIV (November 14, 1931), p. 93.

In the United States there were many who felt that the government had a certain moral responsibility toward the bondholders who suffered from the defaults.[10] They criticized the government for encouraging financial intercourse with Latin America, and allegations were made that the southern countries were induced to borrow from the United States at high rates of interest.[11] This resentment toward the government was based on the fact that since 1922, in an effort to safeguard the public interest, the Department of State had followed the procedure of requesting that all proposals for loans to foreign governments should be submitted to it for the purpose of determining whether such loans would be in contravention of national policy.[12] If the State Department approved of a loan, the investors were so informed, but at the same time they were warned that the government could not undertake to give advice in regard to the financial risks involved. This the investor or banking house had to ascertain through the usual channels.

As this warning was conveyed only to the investing house or bank, and not to the investing public, the government became the target of criticism for irate bondholders who lost their earnings through the defaults.[13] Unquestionably, there were many investors who looked upon the State Department's approval of a loan as a guaranty that it was financially sound. In addition, the American man in the street was unaware of the implications of the Hoover administration's change of policy in reference to the protection of American interests in Latin America. He was prone to misconstrue the State Department's "go-ahead" signal on the purchase of foreign securities as a guaranty that the government would take steps to protect American investors if necessary.

Undoubtedly the government's system of requiring State Department approval before a foreign loan could be floated in the United States aided in the promotion and sale of many of the bonds that were in default in the latter part of the Hoover regime. Many of the defaulted Latin-American loans had been issued in the boom of pros-

---

[10] Toynbee, *International Affairs, 1933*, p. 319. An association to protect the interests of American investors was formed; see the *New York Times*, October 24, 1931.

[11] See the *New York Times*, January 4, 1932.

[12] For the Department of State's statement on the subject, see *Foreign Relations, 1922*, I, 557–58.

[13] Toynbee, *op. cit.*, pp. 319–20; Department of State, "Review of Questions," Part III, p. 3.

perity, before Hoover came to office, and a large number were completed with the government's blessings in the days of President Taft's "dollar diplomacy."[14] Hoover had long been on record as being opposed to indiscriminate loans to Latin-American governments.[15] He was against loans that were to be used for the purchase of munitions or other nonpublic works. When he was Secretary of Commerce, he maintained that loans to Latin America should be made for productive purposes, and he upheld this view throughout his presidency.

Nevertheless, many of the administration's critics pointed to the fact that in some cases the Department of State had given its consent to a loan against the advice of the Department of Commerce. Such approval was usually given on the assumption that the political repercussions would be disadvantageous or damaging to the nation's foreign policy if strong objections were raised to a proposed loan, but was not a guaranty of the economic soundness of the venture.

In June 1930, the Senate passed a resolution asking Secretary of State Stimson on what authorization, constitutional or statutory, his department based its right to give or withhold approval on foreign loans.[16] In defense of the State Department, Stimson expressed the opinion that the Department's action was in accordance with the Constitution and the revised statutes of the United States, and that it acted for other government bureaus. He denied that there was any interference with the powers of the Federal Reserve Board.[17] On February 26, 1931, the Senate passed another resolution in which it declared that the Department of State should discontinue the dangerous practice of involving the United States government in any responsibility for foreign investment loans.[18] On December 9, 1931, Senator Hiram W. Johnson of California introduced another resolution, calling for an investigation of the sale of foreign bonds or securities in the United States.[19] The entire problem of foreign loans was aired in the hearings on this resolution which occupied many weeks

[14] See Thurston, "Relations With Our Latin American Neighbors," pp. 116–17; also "American Loans to Latin America," *Nation*, January 27, 1932, p. 93.

[15] See the *New York Times*, May 3, 1927; *Hoover's Latin-American Addresses*, p. 30; Myers, ed., *Hoover Papers*, I, 29–30.

[16] See *Congressional Record*, 71st Cong., 2d sess., p. 10874. For a commentary on the entire subject and a table showing the number of loans approved by the Department of State, see *ibid.*, pp. 10874–79; also *New York Times*, June 17, 1930.

[17] See the *New York Times*, June 21, 1930.

[18] See the *Congressional Record*, 71st Cong., 2d sess., p. 11647.

[19] *Ibid.*, 72d Cong., 1st sess., pp. 213–14; *New York Times*, December 10, 1931.

of the Senate Finance Committee's time during 1932.[20] Both the actions of the Department of State and of the investment houses were strongly criticized by numerous witnesses. Senator Johnson was vociferous in his condemnation, and in March 1932 he described the means by which some of the Latin-American loans had been obtained as "a little short of infamous."[21] Despite the attacks upon the State Department's practices, the Hoover administration did not modify its view that its "big stick" was not at the disposal of every American citizen who had a grievance caused by the purchase of South American securities.

Early in February 1931, Stimson issued a statement to the effect that the government had no means of affording relief to private investors in foreign securities on which defaults had occurred, and that the investors could only have recourse to the investment houses which had acted as agents for the issue of the loans.[22] Three months later, in his broadcast of May 9, defending the administration's Latin-American policy, Stimson explained that the protection policy, as practiced by the government, was first established by Elihu Root when he headed the State Department, and emphasized that American armed forces would not be used to collect debts.[23]

The financial plight of the governments south of the Rio Grande, and the announcement in June 1931 of Hoover's proposal for a moratorium on intergovernmental debts, which applied primarily to Europe, gave rise to hopes for a similar moratorium on South American debts. The rumors flew thick and fast that the President would apply the moratorium principle to the debts of the southern governments. A week later Hoover spiked these rumors by issuing a press statement denying that the government was taking any steps "concerning South American debts."[24] The big difference between the European and the South American debts was that the European debts were intergovernmental, while the South American debts were private loans negotiated by United States banks and investment houses. Because of this, the South American debts were ineligible for presidential intervention by a moratorium. This distinction between the

[20] For details, see the voluminous U.S. Senate, *Sale of Foreign Bonds or Securities in the United States, Hearings Before the Committee on Finance . . . . Pursuant to S. Res. 19*, 72d Cong., 1st sess.

[21] *New York Times*, March 16, 1932.

[22] Toynbee, *op. cit.*, 1933, pp. 320–21.

[23] See Department of State Press Releases, No. 84 (May 9, 1931), p. 392.

[24] Presidential Press Releases, June 27, 1931.

loans made on the two continents was well known, but even so the American republics "seethed with desire for help," and agitated for a debt-payment vacation until Hoover's statement curbed their soaring hopes.

Though the moratorium was not possible, Hoover showed a keen interest in projects for the rehabilitation of South American currencies, which were under discussion in the summer of 1931. Hoover's denial of the moratorium was issued simultaneously with the announcement that certain New York banking interests would have the co-operation of the Federal Reserve System in conducting an inquiry into the possibility of making additional loans to certain countries of Hispanic America.

The Hoover administration could not follow quite the same financial policy in reference to defaults on loans to the Central American republics of the Caribbean area. These loans were usually subject to an agreement between the United States government and the government of the country concerned. The agreements generally stipulated that the customs receipts or other internal revenues should be pledged to the payment of the debt and should be collected under United States auspices as long as the loan remained unamortized. In a number of cases a definite condition was added, providing for tighter economic control by the United States, should the debtor default. In the past, defaults on loans had often been the cause for active intervention by the United States in the affairs of Caribbean countries, but the Hoover administration, in accordance with its new nonintervention policy, refused to make defaults the excuse for further interference.[25] This policy put a heavy strain on the State Department. For, by the end of Hoover's term in office, approximately a billion dollars in bonds, issued by the national, state, or municipal governments of Latin America and held by United States citizens, were in default.[26] As a consequence, the State Department was often called upon to smooth out ruffled relations between bankrupt foreign borrowers and irate American bondholders. It usually was rewarded by criticism from both sides.

An example of the administration's policy in the Caribbean, and how it worked in practice, is shown in the case of the Dominican Republic. In the latter part of 1931, the United States allowed the

[25] This was important both in South America and in the Caribbean area, but was most significant in the northern section as it had been the theater of past interventions; see Stimson, "Bases of American Foreign Policy," p. 395.

[26] Department of State, "Review of Questions," Part III, p. 2.

republic's government to default on a loan issued in 1924, a period of great prosperity for the island country.[27] Mismanagement, extravagance in government, a large decrease in customs receipts, owing to the falling off of imports, all helped bring to a head the economic crisis of 1931, which had been accentuated by a disastrous hurricane in the island republic in September 1930.[28] Shortly after the hurricane, President Hoover sent a special representative to the island to inquire into the financial needs of the country. This investigator made a special report of his findings. Despite the drastic efforts of both the United States and the government of the Dominican Republic, the island country's financial problems became aggravated. Consequently, in the autumn of 1931, the Dominican authorities informed the United States that they found it necessary to promulgate an emergency law which would temporarily suspend amortization payments and divert certain customs revenues to the ordinary needs of public administration. At the same time, they proposed to continue the payment of interest charges on the republic's external bonds.[29] They found this step indispensable to avert financial disaster, although it violated their obligations to bondholders and was not in accordance with the terms of the agreement between their country and the United States.

After having made an investigation which confirmed the seriousness of the island country's plight, the Department of State notified the Dominican government that it recognized the impelling reasons for the measures taken. It pointed out that although the United States would not intervene, the step taken by the Trujillo regime would necessarily extend the life of the receivership of the customs for as long as the amortization payments were held in abeyance.[30] On November 10, 1931, the Department of State commented on the subject by declaring that the Hoover administration was "not disposed at this time to take any action other than to continue to follow with care the developments in the Dominican Republic." The emergency law was successfully implemented during 1932; a surplus was gradually accumulated, and at the close of the fiscal year the Dominican

[27] *Foreign Relations, 1931*, II, 110–38.

[28] Department of State, "Review of Questions," Part III, pp. 4–6; also Hoover to Trujillo, September 5, 1931, in *Foreign Relations, 1931*, II, 117–18.

[29] See *ibid.*, pp. 110–16; also Department of State, "Review of Questions," Part III, pp. 14–29.

[30] *Foreign Relations, 1931*, II, 131–32.

government announced that there was no deficiency in the national budget.[31]

A later but otherwise similar case was that of El Salvador. Here the Hoover administration again followed its policy of restraint. In February 1932, the unrecognized revolutionary regime of General Martínez defaulted on an American loan which dated from 1922.[32] This loan was not one of those subject to a special agreement between the Salvadoran and United States governments, but the conditions of the private contract gave the American bankers who handled the loan the right to appoint a fiscal representative to whom customs would be paid, plus the additional privilege of enforcing their contract by a customs receivership in the case of a default.[33] However, the United States government was involved indirectly in the loan, for the agreement between the bankers and the Salvadoran government also provided that disputes between the two parties should be referred for a decision to the Chief Justice of the United States Supreme Court, through the Secretary of State. Despite these and other commitments the Martínez government issued a decree ordering the customs duties which were pledged to the service of the loan to be paid into the government treasury. The Hoover administration refused to assist the American bankers in enforcing the contract and establishing a receivership, giving as its reason the fact that it had not recognized the Martínez government.[34]

The reluctance of the Hoover administration to embark upon new financial undertakings in the Caribbean region did not mean that it would prematurely abandon the responsibilities it had inherited in that vital area. Thus, while the considered and deliberate policy of the Hoover administration was to bring an end to American intervention in Central America and the Caribbean, it was found necessary to retain, as in the cases of Nicaragua and Haiti, a degree of financial control even after military control was abolished. This was done on the ground that the administration was under an obligation to bondholders who had advanced money in these countries in the belief that the revenue pledged to the service of the loans would be collected under the supervision of United States officials.

The economic depression created a serious problem in United

[31] Department of State, "Review of Questions," Part III, p. 26.
[32] See Bemis, *The Latin American Policy of the United States*, p. 222; Also *New York Times*, March 20, 1932, II, 9.
[33] Toynbee, *op. cit.*, 1933, p. 322.
[34] *Ibid.*, pp. 322–23.

States–Latin-American relations by affecting the transfer of credits from many of the southern republics to the owners of those credits in the United States.[35] In order to protect gold reserves and maintain their currencies, many of the Hispanic-American nations placed heavy prohibitions on the export of gold. Severe restrictions controlling not only the rate but also the availability of exchange were, in effect, enacted by over half of the republics. Many of the regulations completely hampered trade and intercourse. As a consequence, American concerns producing in these countries or exporting to them were unable to transfer large accumulated balances to the United States. American exporters were also faced with the crucial problem of exchange losses. The probable future depreciation of local currencies made it impossible to transfer funds or to foresee what losses by exchange might come to be.

The depression fathered another problem that directly affected inter-American relations. It was inherent in the drastic decline in revenues suffered by most Hispanic-American governments. These countries cast about for every possible new means of increasing their incomes, and many of the experiments had a direct effect on United States interests.[36] In addition to increased or new customs duties and unorthodox taxes of various kinds, government monopolies were often proposed and established which provided for the confiscation of the properties of American citizens in those countries.

Many governments enacted laws prohibiting importation of foreign articles. This necessitated considerable negotiations on the part of American diplomatic officials seeking equitable treatment for the interests that had contracted for delivery of the prohibited goods before the new laws were promulgated. An example of this was the prohibition of importation of foreign flour into Brazil for a period of eighteen months. The purpose of the embargo was to enable the flour millers of Brazil to grind the wheat they had obtained from the Federal Farm Board of the United States in an exchange for Brazilian coffee. The eighteen-month embargo would have given them time not only to grind but to market the additional flour. However, considerable pressure was brought to bear on the State Department to get the Brazilian government to rescind its order, as many American flour companies had large contracts for the delivery of flour in Brazil, made prior to the announcement of the prohibition.

---

[35] Department of State, "Review of Questions," Part III, pp. 3–4.
[36] Ibid., p. 5.

After a series of extensive negotiations, the Department of State succeeded in getting most of the flour shipments contracted for prior to the prohibition delivered to Brazil despite the embargo.

Many of the Latin countries also attempted to confiscate or absorb the profits arising from properties owned or leased by American nationals. A number of threatened confiscations were warded off by successful State Department mediation. Because of decreasing governmental revenues, many of the national, provincial, and municipal governments of the countries south of the Rio Grande failed to keep up payments on supplies they had contracted from the United States.[37] These and a host of other vexing questions burdened inter-American diplomacy in the early depression era.

Another problem intimately associated with the depression was the 1930 tariff.[38] Although its ramifications were world-wide, its effect on inter-American relations was particularly serious.[39] Long before Hoover signed the Smoot-Hawley Act, unpleasant rumblings of discontent were hard in Latin America over the proposed legislation. Widespread anti–United States comment was spouting from the Hispanic-American press. Government officials, patriotic organizations and societies, and broad sections of the intelligentsia spoke of tariff reprisals and anti-American trade crusades and boycotts, and followed the course of the proposed legislation with intense interest. *La Prensa* spoke ominously of the evil effect the tariff would have on Argentina and attacked the government for not protesting to Washington more vigorously over the tariff issue.[40]

Before the passage of the bill, Secretary of State Stimson brought to the President's attention a memorandum on Latin-American political reaction to the proposed tariff that was compiled from the observations of the State Department and drawn up in the Office of the Economic Adviser.[41] It stated that "if the proposed increases in the tariff are adopted, the political effect on our relations with Latin America will be out of all proportion to any probable effect on our

[37] *Ibid.*, pp. 7–8.

[38] For a summary of the tariff bill, see the *Congressional Record*, 71st Cong., 2d sess., p. 10378.

[39] For a list of the nations protesting the proposed tariff, see *ibid.*, p. 10784; also Hoover Papers, letter to Hoover from John Barrett, former director general of the Pan American Union and holder of high diplomatic posts in Latin America, July 17, 1929.

[40] *La Prensa* (Buenos Aires), May 9, 1929.

[41] Stimson to Hoover, June 8, 1929, in *Foreign Relations, 1929*, I, 998.

actual importations from the countries involved."[42] It implied that anti-American feeling was rife, and that in some states the tariff problem had "taken the place of the Nicaraguan question as the chief weapon of propaganda against the United States." The centers of Hispanic-American hostility were Argentina, Uruguay, and Cuba, whose newspapers carried on hysterical campaigns against the United States for months prior to the new tariff's passage in Congress. A comparison of the reports to the State Department from observers all over the world showed that Latin America evinced a greater opposition to the proposed tariff than any other section of the globe.[43]

The Smoot-Hawley Act, although not in accord with President Hoover's recommendations, was passed by Congress in the middle of June 1930.[44] In spite of the ominous warnings from the State Department and the mass of political pressure brought to bear against it, Hoover, with great reluctance, signed the bill, making it the law of the land.[45] The Smoot-Hawley bill had become a political football, and Hoover felt compelled to sign it because he had pledged a tariff reform in his campaign, and if he did not sign the bill, Congress might present one that was worse. He justified signing it on the ground that the "flexible" provision, permitting the President to alter the rates within a compass of 50 percent on the advice of the Tariff Commission, would enable him to remedy any injustices in the bill.[46] He labeled the "flexible" provision as "one of the most progressive steps taken in tariff making in all our history."

Once the bill became law, the immediate effect abroad was to cause many nations to raise their tariff barriers in retaliation, effectively shutting out American-made goods. Washington received a deluge of official protests on this American assault on world trade.[47] Most of the countries of the Hispanic continent reacted unfavorably to the tariff, and quite a number of them urged retaliatory measures. But few were as vehement as Argentina and Uruguay in their de-

---

[42] *Foreign Relations, 1929,* I, 1000.

[43] *Ibid.,* p. 998–1001.

[44] *Congressional Record,* 71st Cong., 2d sess., pp. 10846, 10849.

[45] *Ibid.,* p. 11826; see also *New York Times,* May 5, 6, and 7, 1930. For the text of his statement before signing the bill, see *ibid.,* June 16, 1930.

[46] See John D. Larkin, *The President's Control of the Tariff,* p. 4. There was some criticism of the President for signing the law as a "political expedient." See *New York Times,* June 16, 1930.

[47] See the *Congressional Record,* 71st Cong., 2d sess., p. 12375; *New York Times,* June 19 and 23, 1930.

nunciations.[48] And in the United States, the tariff bill and President Hoover were pilloried unmercifully. One critic maintained that by signing the bill the President "placed against his record the blackest single mark that it holds."[49] In reply to charges that the tariff was a major factor causing the depression, Hoover pointed out that it "was not passed until nine months after the economic depression began in the United States and also not until twenty other countries had already gone into the depression."[50] Nevertheless, the tariff undoubtedly added to the severity of the depression.

During the greater part of the Hoover administration it was the government's policy to assist Latin America financially. Most-favored-nation treatment was granted to a great majority of the Latin-American products that sought to enter the country and about three-fourths of these paid no duty whatever. This policy was not entirely due to altruism on the part of the United States, but was based on the fact that many of the Latin-American products were tropical and did not compete with local goods. Also, the Hispanic countries were primarily exporters of raw materials, and it was to the advantage of the United States to obtain raw materials and foodstuffs as cheaply as possible. Argentina was the leading customer of the United States on the southern continent, but the United States bought little from her. As Argentina and Uruguay were the two Latin-American countries whose products were in no way complementary to those of the United States, but were rather competitive, they were probably the most affected by the provisions of the Smoot-Hawley Act and were, in consequence, loudest in their protests against it.[51] But as the United States had not been a heavy purchaser of their goods in the past, the new tariff did not greatly alter existing trade relations between them and the giant of the north.

From this it may be seen that, in reality, the new duties did not greatly affect trade relations with most of Latin America; nevertheless, they undeniably had a bad effect on inter-American relations.[52]

[48] See Lawrence B. Mann, "Foreign Reactions to the American Tariff Act," *Foreign Policy Association Information Service*, VI (October 1, 1930), 261–64.

[49] Nevins, "President Hoover's Record," p. 389; see also Sumner Welles, *Inter-American Relations*, p. 3.

[50] From a speech delivered at Cleveland, Ohio, October 15, 1932; see Presidential Press Releases of the same date.

[51] For statistics, see Mann, *op. cit.*, pp. 261–64, 274–75.

[52] For the viewpoint of a prominent Chilean, see Don Carlos G. Dávila, *North American Imperialism*, pp. 11–12.

Politically it made little difference what the actual results were. It was what the people south of the border thought they were that placed an incubus on inter-American relations. It is evident that the psychological and political effect of the tariff was an unfortunate one, but it did not nullify the progressive steps taken by Hoover toward the fulfillment of his good-neighbor policy.

CHAPTER IX

RETREAT FROM IMPERIALISM

"Mr. Hoover differs from other American Presidents in not proclaiming any God-given mission over the rest of the continent or that
the continent is divided into two zones, one of which is under the
protection of the United States."
—*La Prensa* (Buenos Aires), December 5, 1929

One of the most serious and delicate problems in the nation's
foreign relations when Hoover became President was the forcible
occupation of Nicaragua and Haiti by United States military forces.[1]
To Latin America this was the *cause célèbre* of inter-American relations, and to alarmists it furnished tangible evidence of the imperialistic propensities of the northern colossus.[2] Shortly after assuming
office, Hoover made it apparent that he intended to liquidate United
States commitments in the two Caribbean republics. In his first
annual message to Congress, on December 3, 1929, he stated that
approximately "1,600 marines remain in Nicaragua" and "about 700
marines" in Haiti, and that these forces were already materially
reduced, but that he was "anxious to withdraw them further as the
situation warrants."[3] He maintained that the problem of Haiti was
the more difficult, "the solution of which is still obscure." His intentions were made clear when he avowed in the same message that "in
the large sense we do not wish to represented abroad in such manner."

United States armed intervention in Nicaragua had its beginnings in the palmy days of Taft's "dollar diplomacy."[4] In August
1912, American troops were stationed in the "banana republic" to aid
the Conservative government against revolutionary anti-American
Liberals and to protect the lives of United States nationals. The troops

[1] For the historical background, see Dana G. Munro, *The United States and the
Caribbean Area*, pp. 143–93 and 227–71; Arthur C. Millspaugh, *Haiti Under American Control, 1915–1930*; also Department of State, *The United States and Nicaragua.*

[2] See Nerval, *Autopsy of the Monroe Doctrine*, pp. 269–70; *La Prensa* (Buenos
Aires), March 13, 1929; Carleton Beals, *Banana Gold*, pp. 248 and 292.

[3] Myers, ed., *Hoover Papers*, I, 140.

[4] See *Foreign Relations, 1912*, pp. 1032–33, 1040–44; also Department of State,
The United States and Nicaragua, pp. 20–22.

remained on Nicaraguan soil until August 1925, when they were withdrawn by the Coolidge administration.[5] The withdrawal was not for long, however, as revolution promptly upset the country's equilibrium, and the next year, at the request of the Conservative faction, Coolidge poured the American forces back into the troubled land.[6] This marked the beginning of Coolidge's differences with Mexico, and his "private war" in Nicaragua. In view of the increasingly difficult situation, Coolidge sent Henry L. Stimson to Nicaragua as his personal "trouble shooter," with full power to find a solution for the devastating civil war.[7] In consequence of the Tipitapa agreements of May 1927, negotiated by Colonel Stimson, a semblance of order was restored to the country, and American occupation continued with the understanding that it was to "guarantee order, liberty, and property." This was the basis for the occupation when Hoover came to office.

The pacification of the republic, as called for by the Stimson negotiations, was retarded by the depredations of the guerrilla chieftain Sandino, who baffled both the Marines and the American-trained Nicaraguan national guard in their efforts to capture him or his forces. The Sandinistas carried on a campaign of defiance and destruction by attacking Americans and their property, and they resisted all efforts at conciliation. Sandino insisted that all United States armed forces should leave the country before he would discontinue his guerrilla activities.[8]

Soon after Hoover's inauguration, Sandino temporarily left Nicaragua for a haven in Mexico, where he remained in retirement for little less than a year.[9] In a farewell gesture of defiance he issued a call to the peoples of Central America to discuss the Nicaraguan problem at a conference to be held in Buenos Aires, which was undoubtedly an effort to make use of Argentina's coolness toward the United States.[10] In the meanwhile, the Hoover administration fol-

[5] *Foreign Relations, 1925*, II, 636; Department of State, *The United States and Nicaragua*, p. 54.

[6] *Foreign Relations, 1926*, II, 809–18; Department of State, *The United States and Nicaragua*, pp. 55–61.

[7] See Stimson, *American Policy in Nicaragua*.

[8] See Raymond L. Buell, "Reconstruction in Nicaragua," *Foreign Policy Association Information Service*, VI (November 12, 1930), 338.

[9] See Toynbee, *International Affairs, 1930*, p. 399; *Foreign Relations, 1929*, III, 580–90. For varying descriptions of Sandino, see Portes Gil, *Quince años de política mexicana*, pp. 361–62; Beals, *op. cit.*, p. 265; Stimson and Bundy, *On Active Service*, p. 183.   [10] Toynbee, *op. cit.*, p. 309; *New York Times*, April 7, 1929.

lowed the practice of leaving the country's internal troubles to the *guardia nacional* under its American officers. In July 1929, after Sandino's retreat to Mexico, Hoover accelerated the evacuation of the Marines, begun earlier in the year, by ordering the withdrawal of about one third of them.[11] More withdrawals followed, and by June 1930, only a little over a thousand Marines remained in the country.

In the latter part of November 1929, Stimson announced in Washington that it was the government's policy to withdraw the American forces from Nicaragua as rapidly as conditions permitted.[12] The Marines who remained in the country were being used to train the *guardia nacional* who were to take over the task of maintaining order when the United States evacuation was complete. The Marines were also used to supervise elections and to assist United States officials in the supervision of the republic's finances. In the early part of 1930 Sandino returned to Nicaragua, where the fighting had continued during his absence. With his presence on the scene the tempo of the warfare increased. In order to cope with Sandino's depredations, the Nicaraguan government increased the personnel of the *guardia* threefold, but there was no increase in the American forces.[13]

The Hoover administration's policy of relaxed control continued, and in the latter part of 1930 Stimson considered that conditions in the country were improved to such an extent that plans should be made for the full evacuation of the American forces after the Nicaraguan presidential elections of 1932. On February 13, 1931, Stimson made a public announcement of this.[14] He also stated that by June all the Marines, except a small detachment on noncombatant duty, were to be withdrawn, and he intimated that the practice of supervising elections and of furnishing officers for the native constabulary would be discontinued. This declaration came despite repeated anti-United States outbreaks under Sandino's banner, and it was not revised when in the following April a new surge of fighting cost several American nationals their lives. About this time a devastating earthquake also added to Nicaragua's misery. American aid to the stricken was gratefully received.[15]

[11] Department of State, *The United States and Nicaragua*, p. 107.
[12] *New York Times*, November 23, 1929.
[13] Department of State, "Review of Questions," Part III, p. 17.
[14] *Foreign Relations, 1931*, II, 841–45.
[15] *Ibid.*, pp. 780 ff. Bad feeling resulted when some Nicaraguan newspapers accused Americans of recklessly dynamiting buildings and causing the fire to spread. These charges were never proved; see Department of State, "Review of Questions," III, 33–34.

The preliminary withdrawal program was effected by June 3, 1931. From that date there were no Marine combatant patrols in the field; the fighting was left entirely to the *guardia*.[16] The criticism which American intervention in Nicaragua had long drawn, both in the United States and in Latin America, probably had some influence on the Hoover administration's determination to withdraw the Marines at that time.[17] This criticism took concrete form when the United States Senate on January 5, 1931, passed a resolution—introduced by the fiery Hiram Johnson—calling upon the Department of State for full information on the course and conduct of the Nicaraguan occupation since 1924. An additional resolution was introduced, declaring it to be "the sense of the Senate that the President should immediately withdraw" the American armed forces from Nicaragua.[18]

Another important factor was the leading position of the United States in bringing about the Kellogg-Briand Anti-War Pact of Paris. It would have been strangely inconsistent if one of the most insistent advocates of the 1928 peace pact did not put its own house in order in accordance with the principles enunciated by the treaty.[19] As a leading sponsor of the pact, and as the country most emphatic in its protests over Russian and Japanese encroachments in Manchuria, the United States was embarrassed over its own Caribbean activities. The State Department's labors on behalf of peace and nonaggression smacked too much of the pot calling the kettle black. If the United States used troops to force its interests in Nicaragua, how could it remonstrate successfully against Japanese aggression in Manchuria? The State Department's hand could be strengthened considerably in its policy toward Japan if it had no Manchuria of its own.[20] Whatever the reasons prompting it, Stimson's February announcement was highly effective. It was hailed with approval both north and south of the Rio Grande and by liberal spokesmen in Congress.

The restraint shown by the administration toward Sandino was well in line with this policy, and was part of Hoover's campaign to

---

[16] Department of State, *The United States and Nicaragua*, p. 107.

[17] Lawrence Dennis, "Nicaragua: In Again, Out Again," *Foreign Affairs*, IX (April 1931), 496.

[18] *Ibid.;* also *Congressional Record*, 71st Cong., 3d sess., pp. 1360–61.

[19] See Stimson and Bundy, *op. cit.*, p. 182. *La Prensa* of Buenos Aires criticised United States policy as incompatible with the peace pact; see *New York Times*, November 30, 1929.

[20] Eugene L. Hasluck, *Foreign Affairs, 1919–1937*, p. 281.

win friends among his southern neighbors. In his annual message to Congress on December 10, 1931, he showed his determination to end the American occupation of the Central American republic by reiterating Stimson's words. He made known that the "armed forces of the United States" were "reduced to the minimum deemed necessary to the training of the Nicaraguan Constabulary." He "proposed to withdraw completely American armed forces from Nicaragua after their presidential election in 1932."[21]

There was considerable skepticism in Nicaragua over the promised withdrawal.[22] In the summer of 1932, Dr. Juan B. Sacasa, one of the presidential candidates, sent a special emissary to Washington to inquire if the Marines might not be left in Nicaragua for some time after the new president took office. If this were done, the new president might be firmly in the saddle before he would have to rely on the *guardia nacional* officered by Nicaraguans. Stimson refused to entertain this request as well as a similar suggestion by the American director of the *guardia*. He averred that it was essential to adhere to the plan of withdrawing the Marines as scheduled.[23]

After the Nicaraguan presidential elections of November 6, 1932 —which were supervised by a high-ranking American naval officer— the Hoover administration's promise was carried to its complete fulfillment.[24] The defeated candidate, Adolfo Díaz, had at one time received the support of the United States. The victory of Dr. Sacasa, the Liberal candidate, was thus an indication that American supervision had not influenced the result of the election. Virtually all of the Marines were out of Nicaragua by the end of December. The last detachment left on January 2, 1933. On this occasion the Department of State issued a statement declaring that "no American armed forces will remain in that country, either as instructors in the constabulary, as a legation guard, or in any other capacity whatsoever."[25]

This final evacuation terminated an intervention which, save for a short period in 1925–1926, had lasted continuously for twenty years. The responsibilities of the United States in Nicaragua after evacuation was limited to the exercise of supervision over Nicaraguan fi-

[21] Myers, ed., *Hoover Papers*, II, 78.

[22] Department of State, "Review of Questions," Part III, p. 22.

[23] *Ibid.*, pp. 22–23.

[24] *Ibid.*, pp. 23–24; Stimson and Bundy, *op. cit.*, pp. 183–84; *New York Times*, February 4, 1933.

[25] Department of State, "Review of Questions," Part III, p. 23; Department of State Press Releases, No. 171 (January 7, 1933), pp. 3–4.

nances. The United States also retained certain rights it had acquired to a canal route across Nicaraguan territory. Acting upon a congressional resolution authorizing an investigation and survey of the proposed Nicaraguan canal, President Hoover appointed a five-man Interoceanic Canal Board in June 1929 to carry out its terms.[26] Nicaragua and Costa Rica gave their consent to the investigation and to a survey by a battalion of United States Army engineers. Both countries, for obvious reasons, greeted the idea of the new canal with great enthusiasm, but nothing came of the proposal. The board, which reported in December 1931, did not recommend any action in connection with the proposed canal.

The administration's retreat from imperialism in Nicaragua justified itself, for in the following month Sandino signed a peace agreement with President Sacasa. By its terms, Sandino agreed to disarm his men and cease hostilities. In return he received an amnesty, a grant of public lands for settlement, and a program of public works to give employment to his followers for one year.[27]

The other troublesome United States occupation, that of Haiti, had its beginnings in the Wilson administration.[28] United States Marines landed at Port au Prince in the latter part of July 1915, just a few hours after a frenzied mob had dragged the Negro republic's president, Vilbrun Guillaume Sam, from the sanctuary of the French legation and had torn him bodily apart in the streets.[29] The mob's fury was in retribution for Sam's responsibility in the brutal bayoneting of some one hundred sixty-seven political prisoners held captive in the city's jail. The Marines restored order, and later that year, under pressure from Washington, the Haitian government agreed to a treaty. The terms of the agreement gave the United States almost complete control of the country.[30] The United States was to assist the republic in the rehabilitation of its finances, the organization of an

[26] Department of State Press Releases, No. 171 (January 7, 1933), pp. 3–4; also Department of State, *The United States and Nicaragua*, pp. 113–14.

[27] Department of State, "Review of Questions," Part III, p. 27. A year later Sandino and several aides were assassinated by the *guardia* on the edge of Managua, where they had gone to negotiate with the government. President Sacasa, who had guaranteed the rebel general's safety, denied responsibility for the deed; see *New York Times*, February 23, 1934.

[28] For a detailed account of the American occupation, see Millspaugh, *op. cit.*

[29] *Ibid.*, pp. 35–36; *Foreign Relations, 1915*, pp. 474–75; *ibid., 1916*, pp. 314–17.

[30] For the text of the treaty, see Senate, Foreign Relations Committee, *Treaties, Conventions, International Acts, Protocols, and Agreements Between the United States of America and Other Powers, 1776–1923*, III, 2673–77. Hereafter cited as *Treaties and Conventions*.

efficient police force, and the development of its natural resources. The powers conferred on the United States were exercised by a high commissioner and five other treaty officials who were American citizens.

Originally, the treaty was to run for ten years, but it was extended to twenty in 1917. This placed its terminal date in May 1936.[31] The duties of the Marines on the island republic were many. They supervised elections, trained a native constabulary, and helped administer the country's finances.[32] Despite the Marines and their "pacification" of the country, sporadic outbreaks against American rule were not uncommon. With the passing of the years the occupation created major problems of policy, which became more perplexing as the expiration date of the treaty approached. The Haitians had many grievances, but most of all they hated being subjected once again to the foreign domination of the whites. They resented the imposition of a culture alien to their French traditions. In the minds of many Haitians these grievances far outweighed any material benefits that may have been conferred upon them by the American occupation such as new highways, modern hospitals, free clinics, etc.[33] This was the situation that Hoover inherited on March 4, 1929.

President Hoover was acutely aware of conditions in the Negro republic and desired a clarification. On September 25, 1929, he sent a letter to his Secretary of State, suggesting the use of an investigating commission to study the situation.[34] He stated gravely that he was "in great doubt as to whether this Administration wants to pledge itself to undertake to take on the indefinite policies of the last Administration in connection with this island." In his reply Secretary Stimson concurred with the President's idea and informed him that he had given the matter considerable thought "as it is one of the major and difficult problems we are confronted with in our foreign relations."[35]

Hoover immediately followed this up by incorporating in his first annual message to Congress on December 3, 1929, a proposal to "dis-

[31] *Ibid.*, pp. 2677–78; also Millspaugh, *op. cit.*, pp. 75–77. For an English translation of the constitution, admittedly written by Franklin D. Roosevelt, see *Foreign Relations, 1918*, pp. 487–502.

[32] See Millspaugh, *op. cit.*, particularly chapters iii and iv.

[33] See Department of State, *Report of the President's Commission for the Study and Review of Conditions in the Republic of Haiti*, p. 8. Hereafter cited as *Report of the President's Commission on Haiti.*

[34] Hoover Papers, Hoover to Stimson, September 25, 1929; also *Foreign Relations, 1929*, III, 204–5.

[35] Hoover Papers, Stimson to Hoover, September 30, 1929.

patch a commission to Haiti to review and study the matter in an endeavor to arrive at some more definite policy than at present," if Congress approved.[36] A few days after he made the proposal, events in Haiti showed the necessity for a more definite policy. Anti-American outbreaks resulted in the declaration of martial law on the island by the United States military forces stationed there.[37] Clashes between Haitians and United States Marines occurred on December 5 and 6, and at Aux Cayes a Haitian mob of about fifteen hundred encountered an armed Marine patrol, with the result of a score or more of wounded and dead Haitians.[38] Reinforcements were rushed to the island the following day. But within a few days the situation quieted, so that Hoover ordered the additional Marine reinforcements that were en route to the island diverted to Guantánamo.[39]

The disturbances in the Negro nation caused Hoover to accelerate his plans. On December 7, 1929, upon receipt of the news of the bloody encounter at Aux Cayes, he sent a special message to Congress, requesting authority to send a commission to Haiti immediately, and also for a large appropriation to finance it.[40] The House of Representatives promptly passed a joint resolution, giving the President the necessary authority. It was amended by the Senate, and finally approved by both Houses early in February.[41] In a press conference on February 4, 1930, the President discussed the purpose and task of the commission he intended sending to Haiti. He pointed out that "the primary question which is to be investigated is when and how we are to withdraw from Haiti. The second question is what we shall do in the meantime." He emphasized his peaceful intentions by re-iterating that "I have no desire for representation of the American Government abroad through our military forces."[42]

Considerable political pressure was manifested by numerous individuals and groups, such as the National Association for the Advancement of Colored People, and on February 7, 1930, Hoover appointed a five-man commission "for the Study and Review of Conditions in

---

[36] See Myers, ed., *Hoover Papers*, I, 140.

[37] See *Foreign Relations, 1929*, III, 189. Stimson questioned the wisdom of the martial-law proclamation, *ibid.*, p. 192.

[38] *Foreign Relations, 1929*, III, 195; *New York Times*, December 6 to 10, 1929.

[39] See *Foreign Relations, 1929*, III, 192–99; *New York Times*, December 11, 1929.

[40] Text in *Foreign Relations, 1929*, III, 207–8.

[41] *Congressional Record*, 71st Cong., 2d sess., pp. 271, 923, 3040–42, 3091, 3123, and 3591.

[42] *Report of the President's Commission on Haiti*, p. 1.

the Republic of Haiti."[43] A former governor-general of the Philippines, W. Cameron Forbes, was appointed chairman. An independent
Negro commission, which was to undertake an exhaustive investigation of the educational system of Haiti, was also sent to the island
by Hoover.[44] It was headed by Dr. Robert E. Moton, president of
Tuskegee Institute.

The Forbes commission visited Haiti at the beginning of March
1930 and was later followed by the Moton commission. During the
Forbes commission's stay on the island, considerable political unrest
was apparent throughout the country.[45] This commission began its
inquiry without delay, by holding daily public sessions before which
all Haitians were allowed to appear, and it granted private audiences
to those who desired to give their evidence in that manner.[46] It also
allowed the presentation of a case by eight antiadministration groups,
organized into a committee called "The Federated Committee of the
Associated Groups of the Opposition."

After a trip to the northern section of the country, the commission
returned to Port au Prince and resumed its hearings there. "The
commission found the situation in regard to the election of a new
president critical."[47] The tension was so great that the commission
recommended that the matter of the coming elections be settled by the
Haitians themselves. "After protracted negotiations" with both the
opposition and the administration in power, a definite electoral plan
"was drawn up which was approved by President Hoover."[48]

In the middle of the month, the commission left the island republic, and on March 26, 1930, it submitted its report to the President.
The report was thorough and penetrating. It praised some of the
work of the United States occupation officials but did not fail to ex-
pose wrongs uncovered. The report admitted candidly that "the high
hopes of our good works in this land have not been realized," and
gave as reasons "the failure of the Occupation to understand the social
problems of Haiti, its brusque attempt to plant democracy there by
drill and harrow."[49] The commission made recommendations for the

[43] The pressure was indicated by the tenor of some of the correspondence found
in the presidential files in the Hoover Archives; see also *Report of the President's
Commission on Haiti*, p. 1.

[44] See Department of State, *Report of the United States Commission on Education in Haiti*; hereafter cited as *Report on Education in Haiti*.

[45] See Forbes to Hoover, March 14, 1930, in *Foreign Relations, 1930*, III, 204–5;
also Hoover Papers, Forbes to Hoover, March 8, 1930.

[46] *Report of the President's Commission on Haiti*, p. 3.

[47] *Ibid.*, p. 5.   [48] *Ibid.*, p. 6.   [49] *Ibid.*, p. 19.

future policy of the United States toward Haiti. In regard to the termination of the occupation "the commission found the immediate withdrawal of the Marines inadvisable, it recommends their gradual withdrawal in accordance with arrangements to be made in future agreement between the two Governments."[50] The various recommendations offered suggestions as to how the dangerous situation in the Negro land could be eased and the steps to be followed. Two days after receiving the report, President Hoover announced that he had adopted the recommendations of the commission as the future policy of the United States toward Haiti.[51]

The Moton commission arrived in Haiti in the middle of June 1930 and remained there for about three weeks, after which it returned to the United States. In the following October it submitted a final report to the President.[52] The report summarized social and economic conditions, explained the educational needs of the country, examined the existing educational system, and made sixty-one specific recommendations. The commission's most prominent recommendation was that the vocational schools set up by the occupation should be articulated with the national school system of Haiti and that financial and administrative aid should be contributed by the United States toward developing an adequate system of education in the island republic.[53] In its appraisal of the educational facilities, the commission contended that from the viewpoint of finances education in the republic was worse off under American occupation than it had been when it was exclusively under Haitian control.

Largely as a result of the steps taken in accordance with the recommendations of the Forbes commission, relations with the island republic improved considerably.[54] In compliance with the commission's recommendation that the military office of high commissioner be abolished and its duties be taken over by a civilian, who would also act as a diplomatic representative, Hoover appointed Dr. Dana G. Munro, then chief of the Latin-American Division of the State Department, minister to Haiti.[55] The Forbes commission had suggested "increasingly rapid Haitianization" of the various treaty services. Accordingly, Munro began at once to return to Haitian control most of the important public functions that had been assumed by the Ameri-

[50] Report of the President's Commission on Haiti, p. 21.
[51] New York Times, March 29, 1930.
[52] Report on Education in Haiti, pp. iii and v.
[53] Ibid., pp. 65–74.   [54] See Foreign Relations, 1930, III, 238 ff.
[55] See ibid., pp. 255–61 ; Hoover Papers, Stimson to Hoover, October 16, 1930.

cans.[56] This relaxed control followed the October 1930 congressional elections in Haiti, in which the United States followed a strictly "hands off" policy.

The way was thus paved for the Haitianization agreement of August 5, 1931, which terminated United States control of most of the departments of the Haitian administration, except the country's finances and a few services, such as the *garde d'Haiti*.[57] At the same time the military authorities withdrew the proclamation of martial law and technically put an end to the American occupation. After reconciling some differences over American control of Haiti's finances, a treaty of friendship and two protocols were signed on September 3, 1932, calling for the termination of the American occupation by December 31, 1934—about two years earlier than called for by the previous treaty.[58] The 1932 treaty envisaged the complete Haitianization of the *garde*, but allowed the United States still to retain some financial control over the country. As a result, the Haitian national assembly, after a tumultuous session, unanimously rejected not only the treaty but even "the principle" of such a treaty.[59] Despite the nonratification of the treaty, the Haitianization program of the Hoover administration did not slacken, and the retreat from imperialism continued unabated.

The withdrawal planned and started by Hoover was later completed by his successor. The 1932 treaty formed the groundwork of an executive agreement with Haiti, entered into by the Roosevelt administration.[60] Thus, in October 1934, the termination of the long-lasting occupation was completed by the man who had reputedly written Haiti's 1918 constitution[61] and was in accordance with plans laid earlier in the Hoover administration.

[56] See *Foreign Relations, 1930*, III, 261–76.

[57] For the text of the agreement, see *Foreign Relations, 1931*, II, 505–9.

[58] In a message to Congress on December 10, 1931, Hoover expressed concern for the Americans who had invested in Haitian securities. This concern was a cause of the differences over financial control; see Myers, ed., *Hoover Papers*, II, 79. For the text of the treaty, see Department of State Press Releases, No. 154 (September 10, 1932), pp. 150–57.

[59] Department of State, "Review of Questions," Part III, pp. 7–8; *New York Times*, September 21 and 22, 1932.

[60] See Stimson and Bundy, *op. cit.*, p. 184. For the text of the agreement, see Department of State Press Releases, No. 203 (August 19, 1933), pp. 103–8.

[61] In the course of a campaign speech in 1920, at that time Democratic vice-presidential nominee, Franklin D. Roosevelt was reported as saying that "I wrote Haiti's constitution myself, and if I do say it, I think it is a very good constitution"; see the *New York Times*, August 19, 1920.

CHAPTER X

REVOLUTIONS AND THE EMBARGO POLICY

"If we are to be truthful, we shall have to recognize that the Republican Government of the United States, headed by Mr. Hoover, maintained with Mexico relations of cordiality and of irreproachable diplomacy."   —*Excelsior* (Mexico City), November 9, 1932

President Hoover's administration coincided with a period of considerable turmoil and political unrest throughout Latin America. Over twenty revolutions took place during these four years, and the unsuccessful revolts outnumbered the successful ones by about two to one. Hoover started his presidential term one day after a revolt broke out in Mexico. This set in motion a revolutionary trend in Latin America that continued through the remainder of his term, but was most pronounced in 1930.[1] Beginning with the Dominican Republic in February, almost a dozen countries became infected with the revolutionary virus. In June 1930, there was a successful military revolt in Bolivia, followed by a similar move in August in Peru. A popular uprising overthrew Argentina's government in September; in the same month there was an unsuccessful insurrection in Chile, and unrest was evident in Uruguay and Cuba. Brazil was struck by civil war in October, and in December revolution engulfed Guatemala. In January 1931, Panama had its first insurrection, and political discontent became openly manifest in Venezuela in February, in Haiti in May, and in Costa Rica in June. In July, there was a successful revolt in Chile.[2] The immediate cause for this epidemic of political chaos was the world-wide economic depression.

These conditions and the serious problems they posed were brought to the attention of the people of the United States by President Hoover in his annual message to Congress on December 8, 1931. He explained that "within two years there have been revolutions or

[1] See Ernest Galarza, "Debts, Dictatorship, and Revolution in Bolivia and Peru," *Foreign Policy Reports*, VII (May 13, 1931), 101; Lippmann and Scroggs, eds., *The United States in World Affairs, 1931*, pp. 53–68.

[2] Galarza, *op. cit.*, p. 101; Toynbee, *International Affairs, 1930*, p. 372.

acute social disorders in nineteen countries, embracing more than half the population of the world. Ten countries have been unable to meet their external obligations."[3] In spite of these difficulties, inter-American relations were generally good. The administration carried on its policy of cordiality toward Latin America and, in the main, kept aloof from the struggling factions in the south, in the sense of refraining from being partisan to any particular group.[4]

In view of these chaotic conditions, the governing board of the Pan American Union at its session on May 4, 1932, resolved to postpone from December 1932 to December 1933 the Seventh Interternational Conference of American States, scheduled to meet at Montevideo, Uruguay.[5] The reason given by the governing board for holding over the gathering was that more time was needed to prepare material on important questions and projects that were to confront the conference. However, the atmosphere of political uncertainty in Latin America and the ubiquitous economic depression, if not the primary reasons for the postponement, were undoubtedly vital contributing factors.

Early in the Hoover administration, Venezuela fell victim to revolutionary disturbances. The fantastic exploits of its revolutionaries gained wide attention, and impinged upon American interests. In June 1929 a large group of Venezuelan revolutionaries engineered a spectacular coup by seizing the fort and town of Willemstad on the Dutch island of Curaçao and taking captive the Dutch governor and the commanding officers of the garrison. They commandeered the United States merchant vessel *Maracaibo*, and forced its captain to carry them, their loot, and their captives to the nearest Venezuelan port. The owner of the *Maracaibo* requested protection from the Department of State, but the incident had no serious consequences, as the insurgents had allowed the vessel and their prisoners to return to Curaçao.[6]

The Venezuelan revolutionaries continued their spectacular feats for the next few years. In August 1929 they seized the German vessel *Falke* and used it to assault their homeland. In October 1931,

---

[3] See Myers, ed., *Hoover Papers*, II, 42.

[4] See Lippman and Scroggs, eds., *op. cit.*, pp. 53–68; Toynbee, *op. cit.*, p. 376.

[5] "Postponement of the Seventh International Conference of American States," *Bulletin of the Pan American Union*, LXVI (June 1932), 388–89. Thus, the Montevideo Conference was held during the Roosevelt administration.

[6] Department of State, "Review of Questions," Part I, p. 111.

a group of them took possession of the Mexican steamer *Superior* and used it for similar purposes.[7]

The disturbances in the Dominican Republic in February 1930 led to the deposition of President Horacio Vásquez and the establishment of the dictatorial regime of Rafael Trujillo.[8] During the uprising, the American legation sheltered the wife of the president, and the Department of State protested to Great Britain when a British warship was sent to Dominican waters.

Strong anti-American feeling was evident in the Bolivian insurrection of 1930; nevertheless the new ruling junta was recognized by the United States.[9] Similar sentiment against the United States was manifested in the August 1930 revolution in Peru, which brought about the downfall of President Augusto B. Leguía and installed the regime of Colonel Luis M. Sánchez Cerro.[10] Though Sánchez Cerro's regime was interrupted by a series of outbreaks, the United States carried on full diplomatic intercourse with it. The following year Sánchez Cerro was overthrown, but he later returned to power as the country's duly elected chief executive.[11] The anti–United States administration of President Hipólito Irigoyen in Argentina succumbed to a military coup, supported by conservative elements of the civilian population in September 1930.[12] The succeeding regime was disposed to be much more friendly toward the English-speaking republic to the north.

Even Costa Rica, which had reputedly been free of revolutionary disturbances and the blight of unstable government, did not escape the revolutionary plague of the period.[13] After an unsuccessful uprising in February 1932, peace between the government and the insurgents was brought about through the good offices of the United States minister.[14] At one time he had requested the State Department to send two warships to Costa Rican waters to help ease the situation, but the department refused to use its "big stick" in this incident. It

[7] Department of State, "Review of Questions," Part I, pp. 111–13; *New York Times,* August 15, 16, and 17, 1929; *ibid.,* October 11 and 21, 1931.

[8] See *Foreign Relations, 1930,* II, 699–727.

[9] *Ibid.,* I, 415–28.

[10] *Ibid.,* III, 720–59. The enemies of Leguía were anti-American; see Hoover Papers, Graham to Hoover, May 21, 1939.

[11] See *Foreign Relations, 1931,* II, 910 and 922–23.

[12] *Ibid.,* I, 379–81; also *New York Times,* September 6, 7, and 8, 1930.

[13] Department of State, "Review of Questions," Part I, pp. 42–45.

[14] *Ibid.,* p. 43; *New York Times,* February 17 to 19, 1932.

maintained that this would not be consistent with its nonintervention policy.

After a long period of political unrest, Ecuador underwent a change of government by force when, in August 1931, a military coup overthrew the established regime.[15] This was followed by other barrack-room uprisings. In the course of one of the rebellions the United States was asked to sell arms and planes to the Ecuadoran government. The request was refused on the ground that the United States could not deplete its supplies in Panama; instead Washington suggested private companies as a source of supply.[16]

Throughout this period of political upheaval the Hoover administration adhered to the Wilsonian policy of aiding Latin-American governments which were threatened by insurrection or armed civil conflict and of not allowing the insurgents or conspirators, who were plotting revolution against established governments, to purchase arms and munitions in the United States. This practice was based upon a joint resolution adopted by Congress at the end of January 1922, which authorized the President of the United States to prohibit, at his discretion, the exportation of arms and munitions to any American country, or to any country where the United States exercised extra-territorial jurisdiction.[17] While this deprived rebel forces of any chance of getting military supplies from the United States, it still allowed the Washington government the freedom of supplying the legally constituted governments if it so desired.

This practice was also given the sanction of the nations of the Western Hemisphere at the Sixth International Conference of American States, held in Havana in January 1928. It was adopted as a general principle of inter-American relations in the Convention on the Rights and Duties of States in the Event of Civil Strife. The contracting states bound themselves "to forbid the traffic in arms and war material, except when intended for the Government" of a country engaged in civil war, "while the belligerency of the rebels has not been recognized."[18] The purpose of this policy, in the eyes of the Hoover administration, was to aid and support existing gov-

---

[15] *Foreign Relations, 1931*, II, 138–41.

[16] Department of State, "Review of Questions," Part I, pp. 61–62.

[17] The policy was first adopted in 1912; see *Congressional Record*, 62d Cong., 2d sess., pp. 3257–58. For the 1922 resolution, see *ibid.*, 67th Cong. 2d sess., pp. 1085, 1230, 1317, 1615, and 2256.

[18] See James B. Scott, ed., *The International Conferences of American States, 1889–1928*, pp. 435–36.

ernments, promote political stability in Latin America by discouraging revolution, and avoid intervention in the internal affairs of the Hispanic republics.[19]

The day before Hoover was inaugurated, a formidable military revolt was launched in Mexico by a group of military officers against the government of President Emilio Portes Gil.[20] In the fighting of the first few days, the revolutionists made considerable headway, particularly in the northernmost part of the country, where they almost succeeded in severing land connections between the Mexican capital and the United States. The insurrection confronted the new administration in Washington with the problem of an immediate major decision in foreign policy. Hoover promptly appraised the situation and took action on the basis of several factors, of which not the least important was that the existing regime had been more friendly toward the United States than had any government since the days of Porfirio Díaz.[21] Accordingly, on March 5, 1929, President Hoover announced that the embargo on the exportation of arms and munitions from the United States to Mexico, which had been in force since January 1924, was to be maintained.[22] And several days later, civil and commercial aircraft were added to the embargo list.[23] Concomitantly, the tide of the battle quickly shifted, and the government forces were not long in breaking the revolt.

With the embargo proclamation Hoover brought into use the power granted the President under the 1922 congressional resolution, and gave the constitutional government of Mexico considerable aid by selling it surplus war material and issuing export licenses for the sending of munitions to its forces.[24] The moral value of the aid probably surpassed the material value, as it served notice on the world that the United States was on the side of the legally constituted government, and helped prevent further defections to the rebel cause. Along with the embargo, Secretary of State Kellogg refused to grant the

[19] See Stimson and Bundy, *On Active Service*, pp. 179–80.

[20] See *Foreign Relations, 1929*, III, 338–40; Department of State, *The Insurrection in Mexico, March 3 to May 1, 1929* (confidential).

[21] For the four policies the Mexican government wanted the United States to follow, see *ibid.*, p. 341; also Department of State, "Relations Between the United States and Mexico During the Administration of President Hoover" (unpublished), pp. 4–5. Hereafter referred to as Department of State, "Mexico and the United States."

[22] See the *New York Times*, March 6, 1929.

[23] *Foreign Relations, 1929*, III, 354.

[24] *Ibid.*

rebels recognition as belligerents, and his successor, Colonel Stimson, refused to receive the Mexican revolutionary agent sent to Washington.[25] The Hoover government firmly maintained that there was merely an armed uprising against the regularly constituted government of Mexico, which had adopted immediate measures of suppressing the revolt. From this point of view, the rebels had no international legal status.

The revolt raised a number of diplomatic problems. One was the treatment to be accorded fleeing rebels who came into the United States. Washington decided that they would be allowed to enter the country under certain restrictions in accordance with the immigration laws and that they would not be treated as belligerents.[26] There were other diplomatic problems, such as the control of imports and exports from rebel territory, the protection of American life and property jeopardized by the insurrection, the status of Americans enlisting with the contending forces, and a host of other perplexing questions. All these were, however, amicably settled. Stimson's announcement that American citizens who took up arms in the conflict could in no wise obtain protection from Washington against the legal consequences of their acts received loud approval in Latin America.

In the latter part of March 1929, the Mexican government informed the United States that rebel leaders had ransacked and looted several branches of the Bank of Mexico, taking with them about two and a half million pesos in gold and silver currency.[27] It was believed that efforts would be made to ship the money into the United States. Washington immediately had orders issued to the customs collectors at the international boundary to search and detain all persons exporting currency contrary to the laws of Mexico.

In view of the rapid consolidation of the Mexican government's authority, the Department of State removed all restrictions on the exportation of commercial aircraft to Mexico and reverted to the arms embargo that was in force prior to the outbreak of the revolution.[28] The friendliness of the Washington administration was further shown when on July 18, 1929, at the request of Mexico's acting minister of foreign affairs, President Hoover issued a proclamation lifting the January 1924 arms embargo, on the ground that circum-

[25] *Ibid.*, pp. 361, 382, 393, and 402.

[26] *Ibid.*, p. 392; also Department of State, "Mexico and the United States," pp. 39–43.

[27] *Ibid.*, p. 49; also *Foreign Relations, 1929*, III, 368.

[28] *Ibid.*, p. 417.

stances on which it had been based no longer obtained.[29] Because of the aid rendered by the embargo policy, Stimson believed that relations with Mexico had been better "than for seventeen years past." The Mexican newspapers stated, he declared in retrospect, "that their national relations with us have never been on a sounder basis."[30]

Throughout the Hoover administration, relations with the closest Hispanic neighbor remained on exceedingly friendly terms. This era of cordiality was an important factor in the success with which Mexico was able to overcome many of its pressing domestic problems. J. Reuben Clark succeeded Dwight Morrow as United States ambassador to Mexico and carried on the tradition and fruitful work started by Morrow. Before assuming his official duties in February 1930, President-elect Pascual Ortiz Rubio of Mexico gave evidence of the existing friendliness between his country and its great northern neighbor by paying a good-will visit to the United States, where he was most cordially received.[31] Considerable progress was made in this period toward the settlement of the long-standing claims against Mexico by American nationals.[32] The life of two claims commissions was extended, and negotiations were continued throughout Hoover's regime. Through the offices of the International Boundary Commission, the United States and Mexico held conferences to discuss the prevention of floods on their common border, and the two governments talked over plans for the rectification of the border along sections of the Río Grande to facilitate flood control.[33] This discussion resulted in the signing of a convention for river rectification and flood control in the El Paso–Juárez valley.

However, Mexican-American relations also had a darker side.

[29] *Foreign Relations, 1929,* III, 432. A digest of press comment (available in the Hoover Archives) on the embargo policy indicated a favorable response by the American press. The only adverse comment was found in the *Wall Street Journal,* which was bitterly critical.

[30] *New York Times,* May 10, 1931; Henry L. Stimson, *The Work of the United States Government in the Promotion of Peace During the Past Three Years,* p. 5.

[31] See the *New York Times,* December 27 and 28, 1929. Ortiz Rubio was deeply impressed with the warmth of his reception; see Hoover Papers, Rowe to Hoover, January 2, 1930. *El Universal* of Mexico City expressed pleasure over the unprecedented honors shown Mexico's president-elect; from a translated editorial of December 30, 1929 (Hoover Archives).

[32] Department of State, "Mexico and the United States," pp. 51–56; *Foreign Relations, 1929,* III, 434–60; *ibid.,* 496–508.

[33] Department of State, "Mexico and the United States," pp. 57–58; *Foreign Relations, 1929,* III, 473–79; *ibid., 1930,* III, 535–69; also Hoover's Message to Congress of December 10, 1931, in Myers, ed., *Hoover Papers,* II, 80.

Hostile Catholic sentiment toward the Mexican government was latent but still powerful. The antipathy of many Americans toward Mexicans on "racial" grounds often clouded diplomatic relations. An example of how acts of local officials in a federal nation can almost wreck a carefully fostered foreign policy of the central government was the slaying of two Mexican students by Oklahoma sheriffs in June 1931.[34] The two youths, one of them a relative of President Ortiz Rubio, were shot and killed under particularly tragic and highly questionable circumstances.[35] The fact that the two boys were innocent of any criminal intent or action, plus the close relationship of Mexico's president to one of them, caused the affair to be given a great deal of notoriety in the newspapers of the American continents.[36] In Mexico public opinion was exceedingly resentful, but there were few outbreaks of anti-Americanism.

The Hoover administration immediately expressed its regret over the deplorable incident.[37] A resolution was introduced in the Senate, proposing that a large sum be paid to the family of each of the slain youths, as an act of grace on the part of the United States. Congress passed a bill embodying this recommendation in February 1933, and the money was transmitted to the Mexican government in April 1933.[38] The prompt action taken by Hoover and other American officials in expressing their profound regret for the tragic event, supported by sympathetic public opinion and a favorable press throughout the country, did much to allay bitter feeling across the border. But the final acquittal by a local jury of the sheriffs who did the killing, despite an abundance of damaging evidence, did little to help Hoover's policy in Mexico or to strengthen Mexico's faith in American justice.[39]

Another irritating factor in our relations with Mexico was the blatant disregard of Mexican fiscal regulations by American fishermen in Mexican waters.[40] The differences between the American

[34] See *Foreign Relations, 1931,* II, 708–25; *New York Times,* June 9, 10, and 11, 1931. For the questions of international law involved, see Lester H. Woolsey, "Shooting of Two Mexican Students," *American Journal of International Law,* XXV (July 1931), 514–16.

[35] *Foreign Relations, 1931,* II, 718–23; *New York Times,* June 9, 1931.

[36] Department of State, "Mexico and the United States," p. 62; *Foreign Relations, 1931,* II, 713.

[37] *Ibid.,* p. 709.

[38] *Ibid.,* p. 726.

[39] See *ibid.,* pp. 717 and 723–25; *New York Times,* June 28, 1931; Nerval, *Autopsy of the Monroe Doctrine,* p. 305.

[40] Department of State, "Mexico and the United States," p. 71.

fishermen and Mexican officials led to several clashes, which resulted in the death of a Mexican official under unsavory circumstances.

In another important instance the policy of aiding friendly recognized governments during civil insurrections was not as fruitful in good-will dividends as it was in relation to Mexico. Our attitude to the Brazilian revolution of October 1930 reaped a whirlwind of animosity where friendliness had formerly existed. This revolution started in the states of Pernambuco, Minas Geraes, and Rio Grande do Sul. One of the leaders of the revolutionary movement was the defeated candidate for president, Dr. Getulio Vargas. The revolt spread rapidly and on October 24, 1930, a junta of army and navy officers succeeded in gaining control of the capital city, Rio de Janeiro, and forced the outgoing president, Washington Luis Pereira de Sousa, to resign. On November 3 Dr. Vargas was named provisional president, at which time he announced the formation of his cabinet.

Immediately after the uprising began, the federal Brazilian government proclaimed a state of siege and attacked the revolutionists. Its efforts met with little success, and several weeks later it asked the United States to place an embargo on the sale of arms to Brazil, except those destined to go directly to the federal government.[41] The Brazilian ambassador at Washington stated that the embargo was desired because the rebels were obtaining arms from the United States, and bloodshed was promoted through the use of North American munitions. In response to the Brazilian government's request, on October 22, Hoover issued a proclamation placing an embargo on arms shipments to Brazil, except to the legal authorities.[42] In taking this step the United States was acting not only in accordance with its established policy, as in the case of Mexico, but also according to treaty obligation. Both Brazil and the United States were parties to the 1928 Havana convention.[43] This step was unique in that it was the first instance in which the embargo had been applied to a country of the South American continent. Previously such action had been taken only in reference to countries of the Caribbean area or in the Far East.[44]

Several days before the embargo proclamation was issued, Secre-

[41] Department of State Press Releases, No. 56 (October 25, 1930), pp. 264–66.

[42] Ibid.; see also Foreign Relations, 1930, I, 442–43.

[43] See Toynbee, op. cit., p. 368; Department of State Press Releases, No. 75 (March 7, 1931), p. 155.

[44] See Raymond L. Buell, "An Arms Embargo Misses Fire," Foreign Policy Association News Bulletin, IX (October 31, 1930), p. 1; Toynbee, op. cit., p. 369.

tary of State Stimson had announced that, as an act of friendship toward the Brazilian government, the United States would allow it to purchase war equipment from American firms.[45] This was but a geographical extension of the administration's established policy and an evidence of the friendship existing between the two administrations. Dr. Julio Prestes, the candidate who won the elections and who was supported by the Pereiro de Sousa administration, actually lost out in the revolution. As Brazil's president-elect he had repaid Hoover's 1928 visit by a trip to Washington in June 1930.[46] Both Hoover and Prestes had been feted at a huge Washington dinner that was described as having oozed with good will. In view of the personal contact as well as the friendliness existing between the two governments, it seemed proper to Hoover to aid his neighbor in distress.

As the embargo proclamation was issued only two days before the fall of the Brazilian government, it caused the Hoover administration considerable embarrassment, and for a short while there existed a perceptible coolness between the Vargas government and the administration in Washington.[47] However, two weeks after Vargas had been in office, his government was recognized by the United States—which made it the first great power to grant such recognition. This hasty recognition was looked upon by some sections of the press as an acknowledgment by the government that its embargo action, which had been widely criticized and condemned, was ill advised.[48]

In reply to the barrage of press criticism in which he was called "wrong-horse Henry" and was accused of "taking sides in civil strife," Secretary Stimson released a statement declaring that the government did not favor the federal government of Brazil against the rebels, but that it was "acting according to general principles of international law."[49] He maintained that a friendly regime recog-

---

[45] *Foreign Relations, 1930,* I, 437.

[46] Department of State Press Releases, No. 37 (June 14, 1930), pp. 92–97; *ibid.,* No. 29 (June 28, 1930), pp. 340–41.

[47] Lippmann and Scroggs, eds., *op. cit.,* p. 65; Buell, "An Arms Embargo Misses Fire," pp. 1–2. For a criticism of the embargo policy, see Lawrence F. Hill, *Diplomatic Relations Between the United States and Brazil,* p. 305.

[48] See Stimson and Bundy, *op. cit.,* p. 179–80; Buell, "An Arms Embargo Misses Fire," pp. 1–2.

[49] *Foreign Relations, 1930,* I, 443. Some critics maintained that the embargo was not a principle of international law, nor mandatory in scope; see Buell, "An Arms Embargo Misses Fire," pp. 1–2.

nized as the legitimate government of a country "is entitled to the ordinary rights of any government to buy arms in this country; while the people who are opposing and trying to overthrow that government and are not yet recognized as belligerents are not entitled to that right." He concluded by affirming that "we have no personal bias and are doing nothing but attempting to carry out the law of mankind." He also made it clear that the administration did not intend to change its embargo policy. In his statements Stimson also outlined the basis for the policy as it applied not only to Brazil but to all Latin-American governments in cases of revolution.

When Hoover finally lifted the Brazilian arms embargo, the policy was declared to be "in keeping with the multilateral convention" signed at Havana in 1928.[50] Ironically, when the embargo was invoked against Brazil, Stimson had overlooked the 1928 treaty. This "oversight" naturally produced "some rather nasty remarks" when he announced it in the cabinet.[51]

In July 1932, the foundations of the Vargas regime were rocked by a revolt in the state of São Paulo. The insurrection raised several diplomatic problems for the United States. One concerned the Brazilian federal government's attempt to enforce a paper blockade on the rebel port of Santos.[52] Several American ships successfully ran the blockade into Santos, causing the Vargas government to protest to Washington. After this incident was settled, no other American vessels attempted to run the blockade during the period of hostilities. Another problem arose when the rebel authorities requested that their belligerency be recognized by the United States.[53] The Department of State would not consider the request and indicated that recognition "under present conditions would be a gratuitous and unfriendly act to the Government of Brazil."

During this revolution the Hoover administration did not consider it necessary to impose its embargo powers on munitions going to Brazil. Only a few specific cases of war material suspected as being destined for the Paulistas were brought to the government's attention, and appropriate action under the 1928 Havana convention was taken.[54] About the first of September, the French and Italian governments approached Washington with the proposal that all ship-

[50] Department of State Press Releases, No. 75 (March 7, 1931), p. 155.
[51] Stimson and Bundy, *op. cit.*, p. 180.
[52] Department of State, "Review of Questions," Part I, pp. 16–17.
[53] *Ibid.*, p. 18.
[54] *Ibid.*, II, 1–2.

ments of war material, whether destined for government or rebel forces, be prohibited.[55] The State Department replied that under the Havana convention the United States was obliged only to prevent the shipment of arms to revolutionists. It pointed out that to place an embargo equally on material for the federal authorities might well be regarded as an unfriendly act toward a government with whom friendly relations were maintained.

During the course of the fighting, the Brazilian government asked the United States if it could purchase some military planes of the type used by the United States armed forces. After a period of deliberate delay the Department of State approved the release of twenty-eight planes.[56] Aside from this, the Washington government had not sold any war material to the Brazilian government, nor had it been asked to do so. By the beginning of October 1932, the revolution collapsed, and United States–Brazilian relations continued on their normal friendly course as throughout most of the Hoover administration.

[55] *Ibid.*, pp. 2–3.
[56] *Ibid.*, pp. 1–2.

CHAPTER XI

REMNANTS OF IMPERIALISM

". . . . the intervention described in the third clause of the Platt Amendment is not synonymous with inter-meddling or interference with the affairs of the Cuban Government, but the formal action of the Government of the United States, based upon just and substantial grounds, for the preservation of Cuban independence, and the maintenance of a government adequate for the protection of life, property, and individual liberty, and adequate for discharging the obligations with respect to Cuba imposed by the treaty of Paris."
—Elihu Root, 1901

Cuba's strategic Caribbean location and geographical proximity to the United States made it inevitable that relations with her giant continental neighbor would be the most important factor in her national existence.[1] Long before the "splendid little war" of 1898, proposals for the forceful annexation of the strategic island had received substantial support in the United States, especially from the expanding "slavocracy" of the South. When Cuba was finally wrenched from the senile paternalism of Spain, the cause of slavery was dead, and the anti-imperialists in the United States had effectively barred annexation with the Teller Amendment.[2] Nevertheless, by the Treaty of Paris of December 1898, Spain relinquished her sovereignty over Cuba, and the United States occupied the island for a little more than three years.[3]

Before withdrawing from the island, the United States wished to safeguard its special interests there. These safeguards were first formulated and incorporated into an amendment to the Army appropriations bill, passed in March 1901 and named after Senator Orville H. Platt, chairman of the Senate Committee on Foreign Re-

[1] For an excellent history of the relations between the United States and Cuba, see Russell H. Fitzgibbon, *Cuba and the United States.*

[2] For the text of the Teller Amendment, see the *Congressional Record*, 55th Cong., 2d sess., p. 3954.

[3] For the text of the treaty, see *Treaties and Conventions*, II, 1690–95.

lations.[4] The Platt Amendment then became the foundation for the special interests of the United States in Cuba. It conferred a number of unique privileges on the United States, including the right of legal intervention. In this and other ways it acted as a brake on the sovereignty of the Cuban government; and with some justification it seemed to Cubans and many others that the United States had established a virtual protectorate over the "pearl of the Antilles." Cuba strongly resented the Platt Amendment, especially the third clause, giving the United States the treaty right of intervention. But after considerable wrangling, the Cuban constitutional convention of June 1901 adopted it as an appendix to the new nation's constitution.[5] In May 1903, the amendment's provisions were embodied in a permanent treaty between the United States and Cuba.[6]

During the next twenty-five years the Cuban republic had a checkered career. It was alternately beset by revolution, civil war, social and economic chaos, and political turmoil. Under these circumstances the United States did not fail to use its treaty right of intervention to restore order on the island. All through this period the treaty privileges of intervention gave strength and meaning to the influence of the United States over Cuban affairs. In this period also the strategic value of the island became of less importance, as the United States rose to the rank of a great world power. But the economic dependence of Cuba on the United States increased, and she became a convenient field for American economic expansion. Because her economic welfare was based upon monoculture, the growth of a specialized crop—sugar—with great success, she was not self-supporting and had to import foodstuffs. Owing to this situation and her economic dependence on the United States, her well-being fluctuated with the success of her sugar crop, with the sugar demand in the United States and the world, and with the changes in American tariff policy.

Hoover's efforts to restrict American interference in the local political affairs of the Caribbean countries probably met their most trying test in Cuba, because of her unique relationship with the United States.[7] The Cuban situation that confronted the Hoover administration had its genesis in May 1925, when General Gerardo Machado

---

[4] For the text of the Platt Amendment, see the *Congressional Record*, 56th Cong., 2d sess., p. 2954.

[5] Fitzgibbon, *op. cit.*, pp. 83–85.

[6] See *Treaties and Conventions*, I, 362–64.

[7] Myers, *Hoover's Foreign Policies*, p. 49.

became president of the island republic.[8]   He came to power on the basis of a campaign that was anti–Platt Amendment and anti–United States, but once in the saddle, he relegated his election program to mere propaganda for home consumption and went to great lengths to cultivate American friendship.[9] The wily dictator sought to perpetuate his power, in spite of the numerous promises he had made to the contrary. In 1928, by what his opponents maintained were illegal methods, he had the country's constitution amended so that he could ensure his re-election in November of that year.[10] This manipulation of the constitution became the basis for growing attacks on Machado and the rise of determined opposition forces.

In retaliation, Machado strengthened his dictatorship. He forbade the organization of new political parties and ruthlessly crushed the rising opposition, among which were the nation's student groups. He clamped a strict censorship on the country, and carried on a reign of terror by imprisoning, exiling, or killing those known to be unfriendly to his regime.[11] He was able to do this because he was supported by a loyal and efficient army, which he fed and paid well even when other government employees took salary cuts and their pay was months in arrears.[12] He also used a gestapo-like organization, formed in 1931 and called the *partido de la porra*, or "bludgeon party," which was partly recruited from criminals.

Into this cauldron of political unrest President Hoover sent as United States ambassador the wealthy, conservative businessman Harry F. Guggenheim. Hoover had made it known that he had no intention of sending a representative to Cuba who would be an advocate of veiled intervention, such as had been practiced in previous administrations. Nevertheless, Guggenheim was the only political appointee Hoover had placed in a Latin-American diplomatic post. Guggenheim's activities in Cuba were under constant fire by anti-Machado forces and by various juntas and pressure groups in the United States. Many of his critics maintained that his support of Machado was one of the important factors that kept the dictator in

[8] *New York Times,* May 21, 1925; Fitzgibbon, *op. cit.,* p. 184.

[9] *Ibid.,* p. 184; Charles P. Howland, ed., *Survey of American Foreign Relations, 1929,* p. 53.

[10] Fitzgibbon, *op. cit.,* p. 188; also Raymond L. Buell, "Cuba and the Platt Amendment," *Foreign Policy Association Information Service,* V (April 17, 1929), 39–40.

[11] Fitzgibbon, *op. cit.,* p. 191; Toynbee, *International Affairs, 1933,* pp. 372–73; *Foreign Relations, 1930,* II, 656 ff.

[12] Department of State, "Review of Questions," Part III, p. 7.

power.[13] They pointed out that his primary aim was the maintenance of a strong, stable government, irrespective of the price the people of Cuba had to pay for it.[14]

On the other hand, much of the criticism directed against Guggenheim was merely an outcrop of the turbulent times, and it was his misfortune to serve during a period of tension. The delicacy and importance of his position led to a state of affairs where his every act and word were carefully observed, and unwarranted significance was read into even his most casual social relations.[15] Although working under a great handicap, he apparently liked Cuba and tried sincerely to ameliorate the pathetic conditions in the country. He had a good grasp of the Cuban situation and often urged governmental reform.[16]

Besides Machado's rule of tyranny Cuba experienced rapid deterioration of its economic conditions. Owing to the continued drop in sugar prices and the deepening world depression, her plight became one of the most serious among the countries in the world.[17] This state of affairs touched all classes of Cubans, and gradually almost all were united in bitter opposition to the *caudillo's* strong-arm regime. As the opposition was muzzled, it took to underground methods in fighting the dictator. This in turn led to more repressive terror on the part of Machado. He closed the universities, suspended constitutional guaranties, and placed different provinces under the control of the military.[18] Guggenheim, in the midst of these conditions, maintained contacts with both Machado and the opposition, and in May 1930, informally tried to bring about a compromise to avoid open conflict. Both sides were adamant and would not recede from their positions, yet Guggenheim continued his efforts.[19]

Finally in August 1931, the long-smoldering political discontent flamed into open insurrection under the banner of former President Mario G. Menocal.[20] Machado's well-fed, well-equipped army re-

[13] See Carleton Beals, *The Crime of Cuba*, p. 330; Hoover Papers, letter from the Cuban Patriotic League, an anti-Machado junta, to William R. Castle, July 16, 1931.

[14] Sumner Welles, *Relations Between the United States and Cuba*, p. 6; Dexter Perkins, *The United States and the Caribbean*, p. 129.

[15] Fitzgibbon, *op. cit.*, p. 195.

[16] For a personal account of some of the ambassador's activities, see Harry F. Guggenheim, *The United States and Cuba.*

[17] Department of State, "Review of Questions," Part III, p. 3.

[18] *Foreign Relations, 1930*, II, 665–83; Department of State, "Review of Questions," Part III, p. 6.

[19] *Ibid.*, pp. 4–6; see also *Foreign Relations, 1930*, II, 649.

[20] *Ibid.*, pp. 67–70; *New York Times*, August 10 to 14, 1931.

mained loyal to its patron, and in less than a month the revolt was effectively crushed. Despite a legal basis for intervention through the Platt Amendment, and the importunities of prominent opposition leaders, the United States followed a policy of noninterference.[21]

About a year after assuming his duties in Cuba, Guggenheim wrote to Stimson, asking for a clarification of policy toward the island republic. At the time he advocated a policy of noninterference, which was heartily approved by Stimson, who also instructed him to exercise a restraining influence over Machado.[22] A month later Stimson stated that the administration's interpretation of the Platt Amendment would be based on Elihu Root's telegram of 1901 to General Leonard Wood. He admitted that the Cuban situation was dangerous, but declared that troops would not be landed and intervention would not be considered unless anarchy threatened.[23] This was the policy adhered to when the fighting broke out in 1931, and was so expressed by Undersecretary of State William R. Castle, Jr., on August 10, 1931.[24] The Hoover government did not place an embargo on shipments of arms to rebels, an action which would have been favorable to Machado, nor did it make any representations regarding the maintenance of order.[25] Despite this technically correct attitude, the administration's policy was attacked by both factions.[26]

Following the suppression of the revolt, Machado became even more ruthless. He abused freely the old Spanish *ley de fuga*, permitting the police to shoot "escaping" prisoners. On a number of occasions Guggenheim suggested reforms to Machado, but with the loyalty of the army demonstrated, the strong man saw little need for reforms.[27] The reaction to Machado's rule that motivated the 1931 revolt again spread underground, and during 1932 violent outbreaks rocked the island. Warfare between the government and its opponents continued a reign of terror that lasted until August 1933, when it reached a crisis, and Machado fled the island. Even though heavy

[21] Department of State, "Review of Questions," Part III, pp. 8–9.

[22] *Ibid.*, p. 9; see also Guggenheim, *op. cit.*, pp. 230–32.

[23] For the full text of Stimson's statement, see *Foreign Relations, 1930*, II, 662–65. For the pertinent portion of Root's telegram to Wood, see the quotation at the heading of this chapter.

[24] See the *New York Times*, August 11, 1931.

[25] See *Foreign Relations, 1931*, II, 70; Guggenheim, *op. cit.*, pp. 232–33.

[26] See Welles, *Relations Between the United States and Cuba*, p. 11; Toynbee, *op. cit.*, p. 374; *New York Times*, August 15, 16, and 18, 1931.

[27] Department of State, "Review of Questions," Part III, p. 7; *Foreign Relations, 1931*, II 71–75; Guggenheim, *op. cit.*, p. 171.

pressure came from many sources advocating intervention, the Hoover government did not abandon its neutral position.[28] Again, on January 26, 1932, in answer to stinging criticism from Representative Hamilton Fish, Stimson emphasized the administration's viewpoint by maintaining that the Platt Amendment, although it gave a right to intervene in Cuba, placed no obligation on the United States to do so.[29]

A few months later Stimson again found it necessary to reaffirm the government's nonintervention policy. Guggenheim had suggested that the United States make known to the Cuban ambassador in Washington its lack of sympathy with Machado's policies. Stimson felt this would be a radical departure from the government's policy and "would be tantamount to taking sides on a purely internal political question."[30] Guggenheim thought that Machado would respond to suggestions of reform only if they were backed by official pressure. Basically Guggenheim believed that the permanent treaty itself should be abolished.[31] However, this difference of opinion did not alter American policy toward Cuba.

Though the Hoover administration did not abolish the Platt Amendment, it did remove from it the onus of being the lever of American intervention in Cuba. The policy of nonintervention was steadily adhered to throughout the four years of Hoover's presidency, as it was the key to much of the administration's Latin-American policy. The Cuban situation was observed closely throughout the southern republics, and intervention in the island's affairs would have sabotaged Hoover's entire good-neighbor program.[32] The extravagant claims of American citizens were not made the basis for armed intervention nor were defaulted loans.[33] Through all the strife and turmoil, the Hoover administration was guided by the conviction that if Cuba were to attain a full degree of orderly self-government she

[28] Department of State, "Review of Questions," Part III, p. 9; *New York Times*, May 22 and September 27, 1932; *Congressional Record*, 72d Cong., 1st sess., p. 7974; *ibid.*, 73d Cong., 1st sess., pp. 2891–93.

[29] See the *New York Times*, January 13, 14, and 27, 1933.

[30] Department of State, "Review of Questions," Part III, pp. 10–11.

[31] *Ibid.*; Guggenheim, *op. cit.*, pp. 236–37.

[32] As early as March 1929, this condition was recognized; see Hoover Papers, Graham to Richey, March 25, 1929; see also Stimson and Bundy, *On Active Service*, p. 182. A severe South American critic of United States policy was favorable to the nonintervention policy in Cuba and feared that the incoming Roosevelt administration might intervene; see *La Prensa* (Buenos Aires), February 15, 1933.

[33] Guggenheim was opposed to what he termed the "claims racket"; see Guggenheim, *op. cit.*, pp. 125–29 and 180–81; Fitzgibbon, *op. cit.*, pp. 189–90 and 238–41.

must learn to stand upon her own feet rather than to look for guidance or official tutelage from the United States.[34]

Although Puerto Rico was a possession of the United States and was not one of the Latin-American states, it had been the cause of considerable anti-American criticism by the peoples south of the border. Since a majority of the islanders were Spanish in speech, customs, and tradition, many culturally conscious Latin Americans looked upon the Puerto Ricans as kinsmen held in bondage. Because the welfare of the island was the center of Latin-American attention, the good or bad administration of Puerto Rico by the United States had immediate repercussions on inter-American relations. This larger aspect of the Puerto Rican situation was clearly seen by Theodore Roosevelt, Jr., a governor of the island under Hoover. He affirmed "that when all is said and done, on Porto Rico depends a great deal our diplomatic relationships with much of South and Central America.[35] This was brought home to him by the fact that he was "continually getting letters from citizens of these countries." In addition, American diplomatic representatives on the southern continent sent him clippings from South American papers which carried, in full, speeches that he delivered in Puerto Rico.

The islanders found sympathetic and useful friends in both President Hoover and Governor Roosevelt, even though the latter was severely criticized by some factions on the island. Roosevelt undertook a difficult assignment with little previous experience, but before long he won the good will of the island people. He learned their language and tried to solved their problems.[36] He was aware of their Latin traditions and respected them; he knew of their ties with Latin America and tried to make the island a "show window looking south." Hoover, too, was aware of the island's importance as a link with Hispanic America, but first of all he stressed that "Porto Ricans are American citizens living under the American flag. We must help them as we would any others of our own people."[37] He sought to have

[34] Department of State, 'Review of Questions," Part III, p. 12.

[35] Hoover Papers, Roosevelt to Hoover, December 6, 1929.

[36] One prominent Puerto Rican asserted that no previous governor had "gone among the people" as Roosevelt did; Hoover Papers, Luís H. Santaella to Hoover, November 30, 1930. Up to the time of Roosevelt's appointment, no other governor "had been able to make his speeches in Spanish and to dispense with an interpreter when dealing with local leaders." See also Theodore Roosevelt, Jr., *Colonial Policies of the United States*, p. 100.

[37] Hoover Papers, Hoover to Dr. S. J. Crumbine of the American Child Health Association, October 23, 1930.

the health and social conditions of Puerto Rico's children improved and sponsored measures to bring this about.[38] He urged Congress to make larger appropriations for the island's administration "in order to alleviate the distress due to unemployment" and to help the people overcome the "effects of the disastrous hurricane of September 13, 1928."

In March 1931, Hoover visited the island and was acclaimed with enthusiasm by the majority of its people.[39] He was the first President to concern himself enough with the welfare and problems of Puerto Rico to pay it a personal visit. While on his trip, he indicated that he had wanted to visit the island ever since he became President, so that he could become better acquainted with its problems through personal contact. He reiterated his solicitude for the island's welfare by declaring that he "wished to see every Porto Rican with the same opportunities in life to which we believe every American citizen is entitled."[40]

El Mundo, the island's leading newspaper, published a long editorial praising Hoover, the work of his administration, and what he had done for the island.[41] The visit was heralded as building good will among the island's population, which had previously felt neglected. This good will probably had a corresponding effect on inter-American relations, especially when Hoover stressed the degree of self-government granted the insular possession. He pointed out that the people of Puerto Rico had "made magnificent progress in self-government and the establishment of democratic institutions." "The Government," he concluded, "was ably conducted by Porto Rican–born citizens and there are today only three or four important officials upon the Island who were not born there."[42]

The relations of the Hoover administration with Colombia were characterized by a number of problems that were intimately connected with the economic penetration of American capital into that country.

[38] Myers, ed., *Hoover Papers*, I, 186–87.

[39] *New York Times*, March 17, 24, and 25, 1931; C. Manly Morton, "Hoover's Visit Builds Good Will," *Christian Century*, XLVIII (April 8, 1931), p. 486.

[40] "Speech at San Juan, Porto Rico," Presidential Press Releases, March 24, 1931.   [41] See Morton, *op. cit.*, p. 486.

[42] "Statement by President Hoover Aboard U.S.S. *Arizona*," Presidential Press Releases, March 26, 1931. During the Hoover administration, Congress by joint resolution changed the official spelling of the island's name from "Porto Rico" to "Puerto Rico." This was in accordance with the desires of the people of the island, and was the original and correct form; see *Congressional Record*, 71st Cong., 3d sess., pp. 1970, 3789–90.

Colombia was struck hard by the blighting hand of the world economic depression, and the measures it took to overcome the economic crisis resulted in new diplomatic problems with the United States.[43]

Colombia's problems centered around oil, and the efforts of the administration of President Enrique Olaya Herrera to ease the country's plight through a large loan from private banking interests in the United States.[44] Olaya Herrera obtained this loan in 1930. As no public sale of securities was involved, the bankers did not consult the Department of State, as was the practice when the public flotation of foreign securities was under consideration.[45] Disagreements over the loan conditions arose, causing considerable misunderstanding and ill will between the bankers and the Colombian government. As a consequence of this bad feeling, which affected the friendly relations between Colombia and the United States, the State Department took up the matter of the loan with a view to arranging a settlement satisfactory to both sides. By the end of June 1930, after a series of protracted negotiations, the situation was clarified and the loan arrangements were completed.[46]

Soon after this, Olaya Herrera urged the Colombian congress to pass legislation favorable to American oil interests.[47] Previously he had brought about the settlement of a long-standing dispute between the United States and Colombia over the Barco concession.[48] This was a dispute which began in 1926 over oil property involving American interests. The sequence of these circumstances led Senator Hiram W. Johnson to draw the inference that the banker's loan was the price for the restoration of the Barco concession.[49] The Senate Finance Committee investigated charges that the Mellon interests had received the active support of the State Department in obtaining oil concessions in Colombia.[50] Aside from these differences, relations with Colombia were generally good.

[43] For the background of relations with Columbia, see E. Taylor Parks, *Colombia and the United States, 1765–1934*, particularly pp. 467–80; see also James F. Rippy, *The Capitalists and Colombia.*

[44] Department of State, "Review of Questions," Part II, pp. 1–25; Parks, *op. cit.*, pp. 473–77.

[45] Department of State, "Review of Questions," Part II, pp. 3–4.

[46] *Ibid.*, pp. 13–15.

[47] *Ibid.*, pp. 24–25; Parks, *op. cit.*, p. 475; *Foreign Relations, 1931*, II, 1–2.

[48] *Ibid.*, pp. 18–28; Parks, *op. cit.*, p. 475.

[49] Department of State, "Review of Questions," Part II, p. 1.

[50] *Ibid.*, pp. 1–2. Andrew W. Mellon, who was then Secretary of the Treasury, was a large stockholder in the Gulf Oil Co., which owned most of the Barco concession; Parks, *op. cit.*, p. 476; see also the *New York Times*, January 7 and 13, 1932.

CHAPTER XII

SPLICING THE AMERICAS

"It is of the greatest importance that the people of the United States become better acquainted with the history, the traditions, the culture and the ideals of the other republics of America."
—PRESIDENT HOOVER, 1931

One of the specific accomplishments of the Hoover administration in the field of inter-American relations was to reorganize and improve the means of diplomatic intercourse with the other American nations. This was also one of the results of Hoover's good-will trip, since he saw the necessity of carrying on diplomatic relations south of the border more smoothly and effectively than had been done in the past.[1] While on the tour, he often expressed concern over the quality of the diplomatic missions in Latin America. He felt that the diplomatic officer occupied a key position in the relations of the United States with the Hispanic nations and wished to see his caliber improved. Past practice had been to send the good men to the more choice positions in Europe and to fill the Latin-American posts with mediocre political "hacks" and "lame ducks," who often did great harm to inter-American relations. As a consequence, the diplomatic posts in the southern continent were considered inferior positions by members of the Foreign Service, who tried to avoid appointments there. Hoover did much to change this state of affairs.

Early in his administration he signified his intention of revitalizing the Department of State and of removing the political appointees from among the ministers and ambassadors in the Latin-American countries. He planned to substitute "career men who knew the language and the people of the countries to which they were delegated."[2] This line of action was looked upon with favor in both American continents.[3] The *New York Times* declared that to allay the prevailing suspicion of imperialism and develop confidence be-

[1] Myers, *Hoover's Foreign Policies*, p. 44.
[2] Ray Lyman Wilbur and Arthur M. Hyde, *The Hoover Policies*, p. 589.
[3] Leo S. Rowe, director-general of the Pan American Union, quoted in the *New York Times*, January 23, 1930.

tween the Americas was "one of the cornerstones of the Hoover policy."[4] It optimistically asserted that this intended goal might be reached by making "the chief South American capitals diplomatic posts of the first class, as important as Paris or London" and filling them "with men of the highest ability and tact."

Six months after he became President, Hoover reorganized parts of the Foreign Service under the provisions of the Rogers Act of May 24, 1924, and exercised "the powers conferred upon him by the Constitution and laws of the United States."[5] His purpose was to make new regulations and improve considerably the organization and standards of the State Department—which he labeled the nation's first line of defense. One of the more important changes he inaugurated in his reorganization program dealt with the Foreign Service Personnel Board, which was to make recommendations for promotions or transfer within the service "based exclusively upon the efficiency of the officers concerned." Another concerned the functioning of the Foreign Service School in the Department of State "for the instruction of new appointees."

In his first annual address to Congress, delivered on December 3, 1929, Hoover revealed the object of his changes in the Foreign Service in reference to the lands of the southern continent by announcing that "it is my desire to establish more firmly our understanding and relationships with the Latin-American countries by strengthening the diplomatic missions to those countries."[6] He then expressed the hope of securing "men long experienced in our Diplomatic Service, who speak the languages of the people to whom they are accredited as chiefs of our diplomatic missions in these States." He asked Congress for increased appropriations for the State Department so that he could "further develop the most effective force in this, one of the most responsible functions of our government." In conclusion, he emphatically stated that "I know of no expenditure of public money from which a greater economic and moral return can come to us than by assuring the most effective conduct of our foreign relations."

It was during the Hoover administration that the Moses Linthicum Act of February 23, 1931, took effect.[7] It overhauled the Rogers

---

[4] *New York Times*, June 16, 1929.

[5] *Executive Order*, No. 5189, September 11, 1929.

[6] Myers, ed., *Hoover Papers*, I, 140.

[7] For a discussion of this act, see Graham M. Stuart, *American Diplomatic and Consular Practice*, pp. 192–94; *Congressional Record*, 71st Cong., 3d sess., pp. 5389, 5453, 5577, and 5750.

Act of 1924 and provided a new legal basis for the reorganization of the Foreign Service of the United States. On June 8, 1931, President Hoover signed several executive orders and regulations implementing the provisions of the act and making it effective.[8] Most of the improvements provided by the new act, which went into effect on July 1, 1931, were designed to insure efficient operation of the service along modern simplified lines.[9] "Both the new law and the regulations" marked "one of the most important developments in the progress and improvement of the Foreign Service which has ever taken place" up to that time.[10]

In 1931, before the new act was in full operation, and largely as a consequence of Hoover's policy, there were sixteen career officers as chiefs of diplomatic missions in the twenty capitals of Latin America. Of the four remaining posts, one was held by a chief of mission who had nearly ten years of successful service in the southern continent, another was held by a man who had formerly occupied a high office in the State Department, and the other two were filled by men whose understanding of the peoples of Latin America eminently qualified them for the positions they held.[11] The overwhelmingly large percentage of career officers among the chiefs of missions in Latin America was in part due to the fact that "the men who had earned political rewards were not ordinarily eager to serve" there, and because Hoover was anxious to strengthen that branch of the diplomatic service.[12] This was another indication that inter-American relations had assumed new significance under Hoover's leadership.

Cultural relations between the Americas, although not highly publicized, received considerable attention from the administration of Herbert Hoover. When he was in Argentina on his preinauguration trip, the President-elect granted an interview to Alejandro E. Bunge, a prominent Argentine economist and engineer. In the interview Hoover expressed a high degree of interest in inter-American cultural exchange. He informed Bunge that "among the aspirations

[8] For the text of the executive orders, see Department of State Press Releases, No. 89 (June 13, 1931), pp. 457–60; see also *Congressional Record*, 71st Cong., 3d sess., p. 5447. Previously President Hoover had issued an executive order amending that of September 11, 1929.

[9] *American Foreign Service Journal*, VII (July 1931), 266.

[10] See *ibid.*; also Department of State Press Releases, No. 89, (June 13, 1931), p. 455.

[11] Thurston, "Relations With Our Latin American Neighbors," *Annals of the American Academy of Political and Social Science*, CLVI (July 1931), 125.

[12] Stimson and Bundy, *On Active Service*, p. 177.

which have been mentioned to me, that of the interchange of post-graduates, teachers, and professors has particularly interested me, and I shall do everything that I can toward reciprocally realizing such noble ideals."[13] Hoover reiterated this idea in his last public address in the southern continent. This was at Rio de Janeiro, where he expressed his desire "to see a more definitely organized effort not only between the cultural institutions—especially of students, teachers and professional men of my country and your country—but also between all our Western nations." He continued, "We all have something vital to contribute to each other and it is especially from these exchanges and contacts that we gain the respect and esteem which so greatly strengthen the foundations of international friendship." He went on to reveal that he felt "our intellectual exchanges must be expanded beyond the daily news, the moving pictures, and other incidentals."[14]

Soon after he entered the White House some of his aspirations were in part realized. In 1929, the Institute of International Education sponsored a commission of scholars and teachers from Argentina, who visited colleges, museums, newspaper plants, industrial establishments, social-service organizations, and distinguished individuals in the United States.[15] As a consequence of this visit, the Argentine–North American Cultural Institute at Buenos Aires established classes for the study of English.[16] These activities likewise resulted in fellowships being granted in the United States to Argentine students in engineering, agriculture, journalism, business administration, and in other important fields. The Institute of International Education followed up these activities in the summer of 1931, by sending its director, Dr. Stephen P. Duggan, to South America for the express purpose of working to strengthen the cultural and educational cooperation between the two Western continents.

The task of creating better understanding and closer relationships between the Americas during the Hoover administration was aided considerably by the 1928 Havana conference, which authorized calling a series of special conferences. One of the first of these conferences was the Second Pan-American Highway Congress, which met

---

[13] Quoted in the *New York Times*, January 20, 1929.

[14] *Hoover's Latin-American Addresses*, p. 59.

[15] See Thurston, *op. cit.*, p. 119.

[16] For the activities of the institute, see "The Argentine-American Cultural Institute," *Bulletin of the Pan American Union*, LXIV (November 1930), 1105–7.

at Rio de Janeiro in August 1929.[17] It considered a number of recommendations, especially some dealing with the construction of an inter-American highway and the regulation of automobile traffic.[18] President Hoover sent a letter to the congress, wishing it success in its work, and praised the idea of the highway as a means "of further cementing the friendly and helpful relations that exist between the countries of the Americas."[19]

A resolution of the Havana conference created the Pan-American Institute of Geography and History, to serve as a center of co-operation and co-ordination in geographical and historical studies of the American republics. Mexico City was selected as the seat of the institute, and a meeting for its organization was held in the Mexican capital in September 1929.[20] Shortly after the adjournment of the highway congress the government of Panama convened the First Inter-American Highway Conference at Panama in October 1929.[21] The purpose of the conclave was to consider the questions involved in the construction of an inter-American highway, particularly the section extending northward from Panama to the United States. The result of the conference's deliberations was the creation of an inter-American highway commission, whose task was to supervise surveys to determine the most practical route for the road, and to devise means for promoting its construction. A meeting of the commission was held at Panama in March 1931.[22] The Bureau of Public Roads of the United States, under a special appropriation by Congress, appointed a committee of highway engineers to conduct a reconnaissance survey of the best route or routes for the proposed highway through the Central American countries. By the beginning of March 1933 the survey was practically completed.[23]

[17] Department of State, "Review of Questions," Part III, p. 2.

[18] *Ibid.*, pp. 2–3. For a full discussion, see William Manger, "The Second Pan American Highway Congress," *Bulletin of the Pan American Union*, LXIII (November 1929), 1100–23.

[19] See the *Congressional Record*, 71st Cong., 1st sess., pp. 4342–43.

[20] Department of State, "Review of Questions," III, 3. For the history and background, see Salvador Massip, "The Pan American Institute of Geography and History," *Bulletin of the Pan American Union*, LXIV (March 1930), 265–71.

[21] Department of State, "Reviews of Questions," III, 4; see also Pyke Johnson, "Inter-American Highways," *Bulletin of the Pan American Union, LXIV* (January 1930), 45–52.

[22] Department of State, "Review of Questions," Part III, pp. 9–11.

[23] *Ibid.;* see also Department of State Press Releases, No. 38 (June 21, 1930), pp. 325–26. For additional data on the reconnaissance surveys, see *Foreign Relations, 1930*, I, 279–96; *ibid., 1931*, I, 709–15.

The Pan American Union in Washington, D.C., was the meeting place of the Pan-American Commission on Customs Procedure and Port Formalities in November 1929. The object of the gathering was to work on plans for the elimination of unnecessary port formalities and the improvement of steamship communication between the American nations.[24] This was followed by one of the most important cultural events of the year when the Inter-American Congress of Rectors, Deans, and Educators convened at Havana in February 1930, to prepare the definitive statutes of the Inter-American Institute of Intellectual Co-operation which had been created at the 1928 Havana conference.[25] Secretary of the Interior Ray Lyman Wilbur was chairman of the United States representatives. The purpose of this institute was to "mobilize the intelligence and culture of the three Americas by organizing, in each of the twenty-one republics, a national council of intellectual co-operation."[26] The councils were to promote such policies as exchange of students, professors, and research workers, removal of prejudiced statements from geographies and histories, ways and means of making available to all the sources of information in the different countries, establishment of museums for educational and historical exhibitions, and publication of bulletins for the exchange of information. The Inter-American Commission of Women met at Havana at the same time the educators did.[27]

In July 1930, the Sixth Pan-American Child Congress convened in Lima, Peru. The conference adopted a number of resolutions dealing with general principles affecting child welfare. These expressed ideals which no country attained, but they were nevertheless of great value as statements of goals to be reached.[28] Next, the Inter-Ameri-

---

[24] See Department of State Press Releases, No. 6 (November 9, 1929), pp. 59–60; ibid., No. 7 (November 16, 1929), pp. 67–70; "Final Act of the Pan American Commission on Customs Procedure and Port Formalities," Bulletin of the Pan American Union, LXIV (January 1930), 1–15.

[25] See Department of State Press Releases, No. 21 (February 22, 1930), pp. 83–84; ibid., No. 22 (March 1, 1930), pp. 93–94; ibid., No. 117 (December 26, 1931), pp. 610–11; also Heloise Brainerd, "Two Important Educational Congresses at the University of Habana," Bulletin of the Pan American Union, LXIV (April 1930), 389–403.

[26] See Department of State Press Releases, No. 62 (December 6, 1930), pp. 415–16.

[27] See Flora de Oliveira Lima, "The First Conference of the Inter-American Commission of Women," Bulletin of the Pan American Union, LXIV (April 1930), 404–11.

[28] Department of State, "Review of Questions," Part III, p. 8; Department of State Press Releases, No. 38 (June 21, 1930), pp. 322–23; ibid., No. 41 (July 12,

can Conference on Agriculture, Forestry, and Animal Industry met at the Pan American Union in the following September.[29] In anticipation of this assembly the Pan American Union established a division of agricultural co-operation, while a national committee with a similar objective was appointed in each of the American republics. The conference adopted several resolutions designed to promote co-operation in agriculture, including the establishment of a technical board, an inter-American livestock advisory board, a Pan-American agricultural bank, and a central Pan-American agricultural research station.[30] The next month the Pan-American Conference on the Regulation of Automotive Traffic held its sessions in Washington.[31]

Washington was again the meeting place when the Second Pan-American Congress of National Directors of Public Health convened in April 1931, under the auspices of the Pan-American Sanitary Bureau.[32] One of the important scientific organizations that contributed to the improvement of inter-American relations during this period was the Rockefeller Foundation. Through its efforts, vast areas of the Hispanic nations were freed from malaria, hookworm, and yellow fever, and by its example and co-operation sanitary measures of great importance were taken by those countries.[33] In October 1931, the Fourth Pan-American Commercial Conference gathered at the Pan American Union, where at one of its sessions it was addressed by President Hoover.[34] The conference was composed of representatives of the governments and commercial associations of all the American republics. The conference adopted a number of resolutions concerning commercial aviation, electrical communication, the development of tourist travel, commercial arbitration, trade marks, animal and vegetable sanitary policing, Pan-American economic organiza-

1930), p. 24; "Sixth Pan American Child Congress: Program," *Bulletin of the Pan American Union,* LXIV (May 1930), 461-63.

[29] See Department of State Press Releases, No. 37 (June 14, 1930), pp. 306-7; *ibid.,* No. 42 (July 19, 1930), p. 34; *ibid.,* No. 50 (September 13, 1930), pp. 172-73.

[30] Department of State, "Review of Questions," Part III, pp. 8-9.

[31] See "Pan American Conference on the Regulation of Automotive Traffic," *Bulletin of the Pan American Union,* LXIV (November 1930), 1095-104; see also *Foreign Relations, 1930,* I, 297-309.

[32] For details, see "Guarding the Health of the Americas," *Bulletin of the Pan American Union,* LXV (June 1931), 628-34; also Department of State Press Releases, No. 82 (April 25, 1931), pp. 322-23.

[33] Thurston, *op. cit.,* p. 121.

[34] Department of State, "Review of Questions," Part III, pp. 10-12; see Department of State Press Releases, No. 101 (September 5, 1931), pp. 189-90. *Ibid.,* No. 106 (October 10, 1931), pp. 278-81, contains the text of Hoover's address.

tion, and various other problems.[35] Among the important gatherings was the Third Pan-American Postal Congress, which met in Madrid, Spain, in October 1931 and included also delegates from Spain and Canada. A year later, in December 1932, the first assembly of the Pan-American Institute of Geography and History convened at Rio de Janeiro.[36]

Understanding in the field of art, as an essential part of the Western Hemisphere's culture, was also fostered by the Hoover government. In an address delivered at a Baltimore exhibition of contemporary Pan-American paintings, Secretary of State Stimson stressed the importance of artistic contact and cultural co-operation between the Americas. He maintained that "artistic contact between the American nations is essential for true mutual understanding and appreciation," and that "it is on the cultural side that there is the greatest opportunity for further development of the relations between the United States and other American nations.[37]

Hoover gave his full support to another idea designed to provide an opportunity for the peoples of the Americas to manifest their friendship toward each other.[38] This was the idea that a certain day of each year should be designated as Pan American Day, so that the peoples of the Western continents might recall the community of interests, the unity of sentiments and aspirations, the ties of history, and the intimate relationships that bound their countries together. To achieve this aim, April 14, a day of historical importance in the growth of Pan-Americanism, was proposed. This was the anniversary of the First International Conference of American States, which assembled in Washington, in 1889, with James G. Blaine as chairman.

After the date had been proposed, the committee of the Pan American Union which had the choice of date under consideration suggested that the best procedure would be to have the President of the United States designate a Pan American Day, on which the embassies and

[35] Department of State Press Releases, No. 106 (October 10, 1931), pp. 278–81. For a discussion of the conference, see Adam Carter, "A Review of the Fourth Pan American Commercial Conference," *Bulletin of the Pan American Union,* LXV (December 1931), 1237–44.

[36] See Irving L. Glover, "The Third Pan American Postal Congress," *Bulletin of the Pan American Union,* LXVI (March 1932), 169–71; "First Congress of the Pan American Institute of Geography and History," *ibid.,* LXVII (May 1933), 395–97.

[37] See Department of State Press Releases, No. 68 (January 17, 1931), p. 31.

[38] Pan American Union, "Pan American Day. Its Origin and Purpose," no date (mimeographed).

legations of the member countries of the Pan American Union might display their flags and otherwise observe the occasion.[39] Hoover approved of the plan and of the day suggested. Upon learning of Hoover's readiness to issue a proclamation designating a Pan American Day, the governing board of the Pan American Union adopted a resolution recommending that governments belonging to the Union designate April 14 as Pan American Day and that the national flags be displayed on that day.[40] On May 28, 1930, President Hoover signed the draft proclamation designating April 14 as Pan American Day, and on April 14, 1931, the first such day was observed by the United States and all other members of the Pan American Union.[41] The presidents of the Latin-American nations had also by proclamation declared this date to be observed as Pan American Day.[42]

In his address at the first Pan American Day exercises, held at the Pan American Union, Hoover stressed the point that "Pan American Day will become an outward symbol of the constantly strengthening unity of purpose and unity of ideals of the republics of this hemisphere." He praised the work of the Pan American Union as symbolizing the "spirit of mutual helpfulness," which he called "the cornerstone of true Pan-Americanism," and added that the work of the Union gave it "concrete expression in many practical and constructive ways." In this same speech he underscored cultural and educational relationships in these words:

It is of the greatest importance that the people of the United States become better acquainted with the history, the traditions, the culture and the ideals of the other republics of America. To an increasing extent, courses in the languages, literature and history of the nations of Latin America are being offered in the educational institutions of the United States. A similar realization of the importance of becoming better acquainted with the history and development of the United States exists in the countries of Latin America. Increasing numbers of students from the countries to the south are being enrolled in the colleges and universities of the United States. I cannot emphasize too strongly this important aspect of inter-American relations. These cultural currents not only contribute to better international understanding, but also emphasize the essential unity of interest of the American republics.[43]

---

[39] Hoover Papers, Joseph P. Cotton to Hoover, April 8, 1930.

[40] Hoover Papers, Stimson to Hoover, May 28, 1930.

[41] For the text of the proclamation, see Myers, ed., *Hoover Papers,* I, 303–4.

[42] See "Pan American Day in Washington," *Bulletin of the Pan American Union,* LXV (May 1931), 458.

[43] "Address on Celebration of Pan American Day," Presidential Press Releases, April 14, 1931.

This message was carried throughout the United States, and by reason of simultaneous broadcasts in Spanish and Portuguese it was heard throughout Latin America.[44] In addition, it was reproduced in full in practically all of the Latin-American newspapers, thus attesting to the importance of the speech and the occasion.[45]

An incident which in its own small way contributed to the improvement of inter-American relations concerned a bronze statue of Christopher Columbus, presented to the Republic of Colombia by Empress Eugénie of France in 1866. The Colombian government in 1870 gave it to the state of Panama. With the transfer of the Canal Zone to the United States, the statue fell within American jurisdiction. Thereafter a controversy as to the ownership of the statue continued for years between Panama and the United States. In 1915 a compromise was reached, whereby the bronze memorial was placed in Panamanian jurisdiction in the garden of the Hotel Washington, which, however, was owned and operated by the United States government. As Panama's people and officials attached considerable sentimental value to the statue, the compromise did not please them. The Panamanian government felt that the statue should be transferred to a public place, where its citizens could have easier access to it.

The possession of this statue was the source of considerable resentment against the United States. Therefore, in 1930, after a series of negotiations, the bickering was brought to an end, with the United States informing Panama that "since it appears that the statue is the property of Panama," it could be removed to any location which might suit that government. It was accordingly transferred to a public plaza in Colón in December 1930. This event created a favorable impression in Panama and removed another sore spot in inter-American relations.[46]

During his preinauguration trip Hoover also laid the foundations for an all-American air service with the different governments of the southern continent.[47] In his Buenos Aires interview he informed Alejandro E. Bunge that he attributed "a great deal of importance to good means of communication."[48] He was "very much pleased

---

[44] Hoover Papers, Leo S. Rowe to Hoover, April 16, 1931.

[45] Hoover Papers, Rowe to Hoover, May 21, 1931.

[46] Department of State, "Review of Questions," Part III, pp. 1–2. For details concerning this episode, see *Foreign Relations, 1930,* III, 715–18.

[47] Wilbur, *op. cit.,* pp. 222 and 588; Myers, *Hoover's Foreign Policies,* p. 44.

[48] Quoted in the *New York Times,* January 20, 1929.

over the news that there will shortly be established an air mail service between the two great capitals of America and the points between, as well as between all the ports of the continent." President Hoover also expected "much from the perfecting of the services of navigation and of telegraphic and telephonic communications."

Plans for airline service between the important cities of North and South America grew from Hoover's remarks at Lima, Peru, concerning Pan-American airways. In his address delivered there on December 5, 1929, he approached the subject in this manner:

> It is a benevolent paradox that to destroy the distance between peoples is to construct friendship between them.
>
> Every expansion in transmission of intelligence and in daily contacts of our peoples adds to that precious growth of understanding and mutual respect which makes for mutual interest and good will. I should be proud indeed if I might contribute to the furtherance of so great a development.
>
> Therefore I should like to take this occasion to suggest that the time has come when by mutual co-operation of each of our governments it is feasible to secure at once this further important link between our peoples. I am convinced that by a few practical steps in the organization of airways and at no great public outlay we can secure the establishment of this service through the enterprise of the citizens and aviators of each of our countries. It is not impossible that were the representatives of each of the governments en route to sit around the council table we could quickly devise those mutual undertakings by which we would realize such a service within another twelve months.[49]

As Hoover had suggested, about a year later an all-American air system linked the two Western continents.[50] In 1929, Colonel Charles A. Lindbergh made several flights to Latin America to promote the interests of American aviation there and to inaugurate new air-mail lines. In March 1930 the Postmaster General of the United States "announced contracts for a new service of air mail to South America, to include Cuba, Honduras, Nicaragua, Costa Rica, Panama, Colombia, Ecuador, and Peru, three times a week."[51] This service saved from six to nine days in transit to Peru. In October, Argentina and Uruguay were added to the service. A month later, President Hoover sent his felicitations to President Vargas of Brazil on the inclusion of that country in the new service.[52] By the end of the Hoover admin-

[49] *Hoover's Latin-American Addresses*, p. 22.

[50] For data concerning the formation of the link, see *Foreign Relations, 1929*, I, 542–653.

[51] Wilbur, *op. cit.*, p. 222.

[52] Department of State Press Releases, No. 63 (December 12, 1930), p. 446.

istration almost all of the important cities of Latin America were linked by air with all of the principal cities of the United States. The all-American air service, given the encouraging support of Hoover, had in a few short years grown to maturity.

From this brief survey of some of the inter-American conferences and other nonpolitical activities during Hoover's four years in Washington, it can be seen that considerable time and effort were expended by his administration in connection with the work of the Pan American Union and with the preparations for various conferences.[53] At the same time, the growth of Pan-Americanism was fostered by improving the diplomatic corps and the points of contact between the Americas in the fields of communication and transportation. The results of the efforts expended along these lines, while not always susceptible of definitive measurement, certainly contributed to the promotion of better international relations and to a continued cultural and intellectual rapprochement between the Americas.[54]

[53] Department of State, "Review of Questions," Part I, p. 1; see also Heloise Brainerd, "Intellectual Co-operation Between the Americas," *Bulletin of the Pan American Union,* LXV (April 1931), 383–99.

[54] *Ibid.*; see also Stimson, "Bases of American Foreign Policy," p. 395; Jesús M. Yepes, *Le panaméricanisme au point de vue historique, juridique et politique,* p. 156.

CHAPTER XIII

CONCLUSION

"It has been one of the greatest satisfactions of my tenure of the Presidency that it has given opportunity for this Administration in many ways to show its deep sympathy with and interest in the well being of our sister republics."　　—HERBERT HOOVER, 1931

In retrospect it is evident that Hoover's foreign policy was essentially predicated on a desire to maintain peace and had as one of its main objectives the creation of a policy of good will and neighborly understanding toward the southern Americas. Even before he entered the White House, Hoover indicated that he was determined to better the relationship of the United States with our Latin-American neighbors. In accordance with this objective, Hoover constructed a definite Latin-American policy for his administration. He made it a positive part of the government's program to cultivate the friendship of the southern nations and to practice the ideal of the "good neighbor."[1] In summarizing the policy of the Hoover administration toward the Latin-American nations, Henry L. Stimson declared that "we have sought to make our policy towards them so clear in its implications of justice and good will, in its avoidance of anything which could be even misconstrued into a policy of forceful intervention or a desire for exploitation of those republics and their citizens, as to reassure the most timid or suspicious among them."[2] These efforts were not in vain, for it is evident from the results of Hoover's Latin-American policy that good will between the Americas improved considerably during his administration.

It should be clear that Hoover's policy contributed to a favorable transformation in our relations with Latin America, as it should also be clear that inter-American relations prior to the Hoover administration were at a dangerously low ebb.[3] This stagnating state of

[1] See Harry T. Collings, "Importance of Our Relations with Latin America," *Annals of the American Academy of Political and Social Science,* CLVI (July 1931), 134; François de Tessan, *Le président Hoover et la politique américaine,* p. 121.

[2] Stimson, "Bases of American Foreign Policy," pp. 394–95.

[3] See Yepes, *Le panaméricanisme au point de vue historique, juridique et politique,* pp. 154–55.

affairs was brought to the attention of President Coolidge in the latter part of his administration, and in some last-minute efforts he sought to improve inter-American relations.[4] His first step in that direction was the appointment of Dwight Morrow as ambassador to Mexico. Despite Coolidge's previous policies of intervention and the antagonism directed against him in Latin America, this appointment gave a profitable return in good-will dividends. Next, he personally attended the Havana conference of 1928, and appointed the distinguished Charles E. Hughes as chairman of the American delegation. These belated attempts to reverse the growing strength of anti-Americanism and Yankeephobia in Latin America were the first manifestations of what was to be a new era in relations between the Americas.

The 1928 Havana conference marked a turning point in inter-American relations.[5] It was the last Pan-American gathering in which American imperialism was defended. Hughes impressed upon the southern nations that the United States was interested in improving relations with them; and the conference thus laid the ground for a trend of better understanding. Hoover helped make this trend a reality. On his preinauguration trip Hoover explained his good-neighbor ideal, which he later put into practice, to the peoples of the southern republics. Through the deeds of his administration he overcame many of their fears of United States imperialism and of the Monroe Doctrine, and he allayed their Yankeephobia. He sought to substitute neighborly interest and understanding in the place of "police diplomacy." During his four years in the White House, he probably traveled farther along the road of Pan-American solidarity than any previous President.

If Hoover's Latin-American policy was to have any lasting value it had to be a national policy, not the policy of the Republican party. This apparently was recognized by his administration, and the policy followed was avowedly nonpartisan. As such, it was adopted and expanded by his Democratic successor, President Franklin D. Roosevelt.[6] Hoover's Undersecretary of State, William R. Castle, Jr., succinctly expressed the nonpartisan qualities of the government's Latin-American policy in the following manner:

[4] See Bryn-Jones, *Frank B. Kellogg*, pp. 179–84 and 197.

[5] For an interesting commentary on this point, see *ibid.*, pp. 199–200; also Perkins, *Hands Off: A History of the Monroe Doctrine*, p. 348.

[6] See Yepes, *op. cit.*, pp. 155–56. The author maintains that Hoover's adversary, Franklin D. Roosevelt, did nothing more than follow and amplify the policy of Hoover, which he labeled "a national policy shared equally by all parties."

Our relations with Latin America are, above all, not in any way partisan. It is the United States which has duties and responsibilities, not the party. To be sure, the party in power has to carry out those duties and responsibilities, but no government would dare to stray far from the national policy. That is, and must always be, a policy of frank and friendly co-operation with our friends in Latin America.[7]

This was intended as an assurance to the nations of the Western Hemisphere that the friendly and neighborly interest of the United States would not change with the ever whirling wheel of political fortune.

As Hoover's Latin-American policy was admittedly nonpartisan and was adopted by his Democratic successor, it was in many ways the real beginning of what has come to be popularly known as the good-neighbor policy. The entrance of Roosevelt into the White House did not result in any marked change in the Latin-American policy which the country had been following in the previous four years. If there was any noticeable change in the policy, it was primarily in the increased tempo of the program, especially in the mid-thirties, when unsettled world conditions gave a strong impetus to inter-American solidarity. Probably the weakest link in Hoover's Latin-American policy was his administration's tariff policy, which to many Latin Americans was anathema. In this regard, the Roosevelt administration made a significant change by putting in effect a program of reciprocal trade agreements, championed by Secretary of State Cordell Hull.[8] This apparently operated to reduce the tariff, and to increase Latin-American good will. But in its main essentials, the good-neighbor policy had its roots in the Hoover administration; Roosevelt only adopted and expanded it.

In December 1943, the United Press made a survey of prominent Republican leaders, who were asked to comment on United States–Latin-American relations in connection with the charges of Republican Senator Hugh A. Butler. The senator, on the basis of a hasty tour of the southern continent, condemned the New Deal's good-neighbor policy.[9] Thomas E. Dewey, at that time a hopeful presi-

[7] Department of State Press Releases, No. 92 (July 4, 1931), p. 32.

[8] See Cordell Hull, *The Memoirs of Cordell Hull*, I, 81–85 and 357–60.

[9] Butler attacked the good-neighbor policy as being "a hemispheric handout that is neither good nor neighborly"; see Hugh A. Butler, "Our Deep Dark Secrets in Latin America," *Reader's Digest*, XLIII (December 1943), 21. For a discussion of Butler's charges, see "Butler's Boondoggles," *Newsweek*, XXII (December 27, 1943), p. 42.

dential prospect, stated that there "was no partisanship in the United States regarding the good-neighbor policy," and that it had been established during Republican administrations.[10] America's senior statesman and former President, Herbert Hoover, commented on the same subject by reviewing his accomplishments in the field of inter-American relations, his use of the term "good neighbor," and his reversal of the nation's practice of intervention. He pointed out that he had emphasized nonintervention throughout his administration and that he had given proof of his intentions by withdrawing the Marines from Nicaragua and the occupation troops from Haiti. He concluded by stating that he "was happy to say that it was the last of these interventions and the last of the policy of American interference in the domestic policies of the Latin-American States."[11]

Sumner Welles, who was one of the principal architects of Franklin D. Roosevelt's Latin-American policy, took exception to Hoover's claims "for the paternity of the good-neighbor policy."[12] He contended that Hoover's policies were well-intentioned and were steps in the right direction, but that they failed for two reasons. The first was that Hoover had served for eight years in the cabinets of Harding and Coolidge, which, Latin Americans felt, tinged him with interventionist relationships. The second was that "only a year after Mr. Hoover assumed office he signed the Smoot-Hawley Tariff Act." Even though Hoover's good-neighbor policy might well lay claim to being nonpartisan, its results have been subject to debate in the political arena.

As to the origin of the term "good neighbor," there should be little ground for dispute. It is a phrase which has undoubtedly been used by many statesmen on numerous occasions. As early as the year 1815, prior to complete Latin-American independence, the term or its equivalent was used in reference to Western Hemisphere relations. The term "good neighborliness" (*buena vecindad*) as applied to international relations was a common one in the Spanish correspondence of the early 1800's.[13] The Spanish minister to the United States of that period, Don Luis de Onís, used the phrase in reference to the attitude of the United States toward the struggling and estranged colonies of Spain.

[10] *New York Times,* December 13, 1943.
[11] *Ibid.*
[12] Welles, *The Time for Decision,* p. 190.
[13] Arthur P. Whitaker, *The United States and the Independence of Latin America,* p. 113.

In its modern sense, Elihu Root had used the phrase as far back as 1907 in relation to Santo Domingo.[14] Hoover applied the term to Latin-American affairs in several of his addresses while on his good-will tour in 1928. President Franklin D. Roosevelt first availed himself of the phrase in his inaugural address and made it applicable to the foreign relations of the United States throughout the world. It was not at first intended to apply solely to inter-American relations, but "more by chance than by deliberate intent" it came to mean the policy pursued by the United States government in its dealings with the twenty other republics of the Western Hemisphere. In the course of time its broader meaning was lost, and it was applied only to inter-American relations.[15] From this, it can be seen that the concept of the "good neighbor" was not original with either Hoover or Roosevelt. Hoover even before he was inaugurated applied the good-neighbor ideal specifically to Latin America, whereas Roosevelt appropriated the same concept and gave it world-wide application. As such things happen, the term has become popularly associated with Roosevelt and inter-American relations.

From the day he accepted the Republican party's nomination for President to the day he left the White House, the Quaker statesman's words and actions, reflected his avowed objectives of peace and good will and his endeavor to fulfill the good-neighbor ideal in regard to Latin America. His good-neighbor policy did much to bring the Americas closer together; it contributed to the elimination of some of the "sore spots" in inter-American relations; it helped to overcome some of the fears and hates aroused by the policies of previous administrations; and it laid the foundation for a Latin-American policy . that paid rich dividends in the crisis of World War II.[16] Thus, in any study of the building of the modern Latin-American policy of the United States, Hoover justly merits recognition as one of its important architects.

[14] See Philip C. Jessup, *Elihu Root*, I, 563.
[15] Welles, *The Time for Decision,* pp. 192–93.
[16] See Nevins, "President Hoover's Record." Though highly critical of the Hoover administration, Nevins maintained that "on the whole Mr. Hoover's record in regard to Latin America is excellent."

BIBLIOGRAPHY

BIBLIOGRAPHICAL INTRODUCTION

In general, the more essential and useful materials for this study were found in the Herbert Hoover Archives of the Hoover Library on War, Revolution, and Peace at Stanford University, Stanford, California. The writer was especially fortunate in being allowed the unrestricted use of Mr. Hoover's private papers and presidential files pertaining to Latin-American affairs. The materials there were extensive and hitherto unused. The Stanford University Library, the Columbus Memorial Library in the Pan American Union, the Library of Congress, especially the newspaper collection, and the Historical Division of the Department of State all proved highly useful, since they contain much that is invaluable in a study of this nature. The library of the University of California at Berkeley is also rich in Latin-American material covering this period.

Samuel F. Bemis and Grace G. Griffin's *Guide to the Diplomatic History of the United States, 1775–1921* (Washington, D.C., 1935) is a complete guide for background material, but more useful for this study were William L. Langer and Hamilton F. Armstrong, editors, *Foreign Affairs Bibliography* (New York, 1933), covering the period 1919–1932, and Robert G. Woolbert, editor, *Foreign Affairs Bibliography* (New York, 1945), covering the period 1932–1942. Most valuable among the published documentary collections was the Department of State, *Papers Relating to the Foreign Relations of the United States* (Washington, D.C., 1861–1948), annual volumes which contain selections from American diplomatic correspondences, with large sections devoted to the Latin-American countries. The volumes most heavily relied upon were those covering the period 1912–1932. The Department of State Press Releases, the publications of the Latin-American and Mexican Divisions of the Department of State, and various other government publications, such as the reports of committees of the Senate and the House of Representatives, executive documents, and the *Congressional Record*, were all necessary tools for a study of this nature.

In many ways one of the most valuable periodicals used was the *Bulletin of the Pan American Union* (issued monthly). Of incalculable value was the *New York Times,* which was used more than any other newspaper; for Latin America, *La Prensa* (Buenos Aires) was the most consulted newspaper. Samuel F. Bemis, *The Latin American Policy of the United States* (New York, 1943), is an excellent secondary aid, and Arnold J. Toynbee, *Survey of International Affairs* (London, annual publication since 1925), as indicated by

Henry L. Stimson in his memoirs, is about the best and most complete survey of the foreign policies of the Hoover administration. Basic is Henry L. Stimson and McGeorge Bundy, *On Active Service in Peace and War* (New York, 1948). This was especially valuable as it is based on Stimson's voluminous and carefully kept diaries.

MANUSCRIPTS AND UNPUBLISHED DOCUMENTS[1]

DEPARTMENT OF STATE. "Relations Between the United States and Mexico During the Administration of President Hoover." Washington, D.C., 1933.

————. "Review of Questions of Major Interest in the Relations of the United States with the Latin American Countries, 1929–1933." Washington, D.C., 1933.

HOOVER PAPERS AND PRESIDENTIAL FILES.

Akerson, George. Letter to Edwin Freeland, May 15, 1929.

Barrett, John. Letter to President Hoover, July 17, 1929.

Cotton, Joseph P. Letter to President Hoover, April 8, 1930.

Cuban Patriotic League. Letter to William R. Castle, July 16, 1931.

Culbertson, W. S. Letter to President Hoover, May 13, 1929.

Forbes, Cameron W. Letter to President Hoover, March 8, 1930.

Grahame, Warren C. Letters to Lawrence Richey, March 25 and May 21, 1929.

Hoover, Herbert C. Letter to Dr. S. J. Crumbine, October 23, 1930.

————. Letters to Henry L. Stimson, September 25, 1929, and June 26, 1930.

————. "Press Statement for South American Papers," March 9, 1921 (mimeographed).

Kellogg, Frank B. Letter to President Hoover, March 5, 1929.

Moore, Alexander P. Letters to President Hoover, May 3 and June 7, 1929.

Roosevelt, Theodore, Jr. Letter to President Hoover, December 6, 1929.

Rowe, Leo S. Letters to President Hoover, December 10, 1929; January 2, 1930; April 16 and May 21, 1931.

Santaella, Luís H. Letter to President Hoover, November 30, 1930.

Stimson, Henry L. Letters to President Hoover, September 30, 1929; May 28, June 25, and October 16, 1930.

[1] All these documents are in the Herbert Hoover Archives at the Hoover Library on War, Revolution, and Peace, Stanford University, Stanford, California.

DOCUMENTS
PUBLISHED BY THE GOVERNMENT OF THE UNITED STATES[2]

Addresses Delivered During the Visit of Herbert Hoover, President-elect of the United States, to Central and South America, November–December 1928. Washington, D.C.: Pan American Union, 1929.

Annals of Congress, 1789–1824. Washington, D.C.: Gales and Seaton, 1834–1856.

CLARK, J. REUBEN. *Memorandum on the Monroe Doctrine.* Department of State, 1930.

Congressional Record. 55th Cong., 2d sess.; 56th Cong., 2d sess.; 58th Cong., 3d sess.; 59th Cong., 1st sess.; 62d Cong., 2d sess.; 67th Cong., 2d sess.; 69th Cong., 2d sess.; 70th Cong., 2d sess.; 71st Cong., 1st, 2d, and 3d sess.; 72d Cong., 1st sess.; 73d Cong., 1st and special sessions.

Convention for the Establishment of the International Commission of Inquiry, December 4, 1922, to February 7, 1923 (Conference on Central American Affairs). Department of State, Treaty Series, No. 717, 1923.

DEPARTMENT OF STATE PRESS RELEASES. Nos. 6–7 (1929); Nos. 21–22, 37–39, 41–42, 50, 56, 62–63 (1930); Nos. 68, 75, 82, 84, 89, 92, 101, 106, 117, 174 (1931); Nos. 119, 149, 154, (1932); Nos. 171, 179, 185, 203 (1933).

Executive Order. No. 5189, September 11, 1929.

Insurrection in Mexico, March 3 to May 1, 1929, The. Department of State, 1929 (confidential).

Inter-American Congress of Rectors, Deans, and Educators in General, Havana, Cuba, February 20–23, 1930. Report of the Chairman of the Delegation of the United States. Department of State, Conference Series, No. 8, 1931.

Papers Relating to the Foreign Relations of the United States. Department of State, 1861–1948.

PORTO RICO. *Thirtieth Annual Report of the Governor of Porto Rico . . . .* H. Doc. 545. 71st Cong., 3d sess., Vol. 2, p. 9352, 1930.

PRESIDENTIAL PRESS RELEASES. March 24, March 26, April 14, and June 27, 1931; and October 15, 1932.

Report of the President's Commission for the Study and Review of Conditions in the Republic of Haiti. Department of State, Latin American Series, No. 2, 1930.

Report of the United States Commission on Education in Haiti. Department of State, Latin American Series, No. 5, 1931.

[2] With the exception of the first two entries all documents under this title were published by the Government Printing Office and therefore this imprint and Washington, D.C., are omitted from the citations.

SENATE, COMMITTEE ON FINANCE. *Sale of Foreign Bonds or Securities in the United States. Hearings Before the Committee on Finance . . . . Pursuant to S. Res. 19.* 72d Cong., 1st sess., 1931.

SENATE, COMMITTEE ON FOREIGN RELATIONS. *Treaties, Conventions, International Acts, Protocols and Agreements Between the United States and Other Powers, 1776–1909.* Vols. I and II edited by William M. Malloy. *S. Doc. 357*, 61st Cong., 2d sess., Vol. 10, 1910.

———. *Treaties, Conventions, International Acts, Protocols and Agreements Between the United States and Other Powers, 1910–1923.* Vol. III edited by C. F. Redmond. *S. Doc. 348*, 67th Cong., 4th sess., Vol. 8, 1923.

STIMSON, HENRY L. *The United States and the Other American Republics.* Department of State, Latin American Series, No. 4, 1931.

———. *The Work of the United States Government in the Promotion of Peace During the Past Three Years.* Department of State, 1932.

The United States and Nicaragua: A Survey of the Relations from 1909 to 1932. Department of State, Latin American Series, No. 6, 1932.

WELLES, SUMNER. *Inter-American Relations.* Department of State, Latin American Series, No. 8, 1934.

———. *Relations Between the United States and Cuba.* Department of State, Latin American Series, No. 7, 1934.

PUBLISHED BY OTHER GOVERNMENTS

CHILE. *Tacna-Arica Arbitration. The Appendix to the Case of the Republic of Chile.* Washington, D.C., 1923.

———. *Tacna-Arica. Fallo arbitral.* Santiago, Chile, 1925.

GREAT BRITAIN, FOREIGN OFFICE. *British and Foreign State Papers, 1882–1883.* London, 1891.

GUATEMALA. *Arbitraje de límites entre Guatemala y Honduras; alegato presentada por Guatemala ante el tribunal de arbitraje integrado por el honorable Charles Evans Hughes, presidente de la Corte suprema de justicia de los Estados Unidos de América, honorable Luís Castro Ureña, de Costa Rica, y honorable Emilio Billo Codesido, de Chile, bajo las estipulaciones del tratado de 16 julio de 1930.* Washington, D.C., 1932.

GUATEMALA, MINISTRY OF FOREIGN AFFAIRS. *The Boundary Dispute Between Guatemala and Honduras.* Guatemala, 1928.

LEAGUE OF NATIONS, CHACO COMMISSION. *Dispute Between Bolivia and Paraguay.* League of Nations Publications, Series VII, Political, No. 1, Geneva, 1934.

LEAGUE OF NATIONS, COUNCIL. *Dispute Between Colombia and Peru.* League of Nations Publications, Series VII, Political, No. 3, Geneva, 1933.

PERU. *Arbitration Between Peru and Chile. The Countercase of Peru.* Washington, D.C., 1923.

——. *Arbitration Between Peru and Chile. Appendix to the Countercase of Peru in the Matter of the Controversy Arising Out of the Question of the Pacific.* Washington, D.C., 1924.

PUERTO RICO, LA LEGISLATURA DE. *23 de marzo—año 1931. Homenaje de la legislatura a su excelencia Herbert Hoover, presidente de los Estados Unidos, con motivo de su visita a Puerto Rico.* San Juan, Puerto Rico, 1931.

SPECIAL BOUNDARY TRIBUNAL (GUATEMALA-HONDURAS BOUNDARY ARBITRATION). *Opinion and Award.* Washington, D.C., 1933.

NEWSPAPERS

Buenos Aires Herald. Buenos Aires, 1928–1929.

Christian Science Monitor. Boston, 1920–1933.

Nación, La. Buenos Aires, 1928–1929.

Nación, La. Santiago, Chile, 1928–1929.

New York Evening Post. New York, 1928.

New York Times. New York, 1920–1948.

Nueva Prensa, La. San José, Costa Rica, 1928.

País, El. Montevideo, Uruguay, 1928.

Paiz, O. Rio de Janeiro, 1928.

Palo Alto Times. Palo Alto, Calif., 1927–1929.

Prensa, La. Buenos Aires, 1927–1934.

San Diego Sun. San Diego, Calif., 1927–1929.

United States Daily. Washington, D.C., 1920–1933.

Universal, El. Mexico City, 1929.

Washington Daily News. Washington, D.C., 1948.

Washington Star. Washington, D.C., 1928–1930.

PERIODICALS, MAGAZINES, AND SERIALS

Aconcagua, 1928. Buenos Aires.

American Economic Review, 1920–1933. Princeton, N.J.

American Foreign Service Journal, 1927–1934. Washington, D.C.

American Journal of International Law, 1928–1933. New York.

Anales de la facultad de ciencias jurídicas y sociales de la Plata, 1930. La Plata, Argentina.

Annals of the American Academy of Political and Social Science, 1928–1933, Philadelphia.

Argentina, 1928–1929. Washington, D.C.

Atlantic Monthly, 1920–1933. Boston.

Bulletin of International News, 1928–1933. London.

Bulletin of the Pan American Union, 1928–1933. Washington, D.C.

Business Week, 1929–1933. Greenwich, Conn.

Christian Century, 1926–1933. Chicago.

Commonweal, 1924–1933. New York.

Current History, 1920–1933. New York.

Foreign Affairs, 1922–1933. New York.

Foreign Policy Association Information Service, 1928–1931. New York.

Foreign Policy Bulletin, 1931–1933. New York.

Foreign Policy News Bulletin, 1928–1931. New York.

Foreign Policy Reports, 1931–1933. New York.

Fortune, 1930–1933. Jersey City, N.J.

Forum, 1928–1933. New York.

Literary Digest, 1920–1938. New York.

Living Age, 1920–1933. Boston.

Nation, 1928–1933. New York.

New Republic, 1920–1933. New York.

Newsweek, 1933–1948. New York.

Outlook, 1920–1932. New York.

Pan American Magazine, 1928–1931. Washington, D.C.

Political Science Quarterly, 1920–1933. Boston.

Reader's Digest, 1941–1945. Pleasantville, N.Y.

Review of Reviews, 1920–1933. New York.

Saturday Evening Post, 1928–1933. Philadelphia.

South Atlantic Quarterly, The, 1935. Durham, N.C.

Time, 1923–1946. New York.

Transactions of the Grotius Society, 1929–1930. London.

World Tomorrow, 1920–1933. New York.

World's Work, 1920–1932. New York.

Yale Review, 1928–1933. New Haven, Conn.

ARTICLES AND PAMPHLETS

"American Loans to Latin America," *Nation*, CXXXIV (January 27, 1932), 93.

ANDERSON, CHANDLER P. "Our Policy of Non-Recognition in Central America," *American Journal of International Law,* XXV (April 1931), 298–301.

"The Argentine-American Cultural Institute," *Bulletin of the Pan American Union,* LXIV (November 1930), 1105–7.

BELLEGARDE, D. "Inter-American Economic Policy," *Annals of the American Academy of Political and Social Science,* CL (July 1930), 186–91.

BRAINERD, HELOISE, "Intellectual Co-operation Between the Americas," *Bulletin of the Pan American Union,* LXV (April 1931), 383–99.

———. "Two Important Educational Congresses at the University of Habana," *ibid.,* LXIV (April 1930), 389–403.

BROWN, PHILIP M. "The Recognition of New Governments," *American Journal of International Law,* XXVI (April 1932), 336–40.

BUELL, RAYMOND L. "The American Occupation of Haiti," *Foreign Policy Association Information Service,* V (November 27 and December 12, 1929), 327–92.

———. "American Supervision of Elections in Nicaragua," *ibid.,* VI (December 24, 1930), 385–402.

———. "An Arms Embargo Misses Fire," *Foreign Policy Association News Bulletin,* IX (October 31, 1930).

———. "The Caribbean Situation: Cuba and Haiti," *Foreign Policy Reports,* IX (June 21, 1933), 82–92.

———. "Changes in Our Latin American Policy," *Annals of the American Academy of Political and Social Science,* CLVI (July 1931), 126–32.

———. "Cuba and the Platt Amendment," *Foreign Policy Association Information Service,* V (April 17, 1929), 37–62.

———. "Getting Out of Central America," *Nation,* CXXXV (July 13, 1932), 32–34.

———. "New Latin American Policy," *Forum,* LXXXI (February 1929), 113–18.

———. "Panama and the United States," *Foreign Policy Reports,* VII (January 20, 1932), 409–26.

———. "Reconstruction in Nicaragua," *Foreign Policy Association Information Service,* VI (November 12, 1930), 315–43.

———. "The United States and Central American Revolutions," *Foreign Policy Reports,* VII (July 22, 1931), 187–204.

———. "The United States and Central American Stability," *ibid.,* VII (July 8, 1931), 161–86.

———. "The United States and Latin America," *Foreign Policy Association Information Service,* III (January 1928) special supplement, 77–94.

Butler, Hugh A. "Our Deep Dark Secrets in Latin America," *Reader's Digest*, XLII (December 1943), 21–25.

————. "They Are Still Deep Dark Secrets," *ibid.*, XLIV (February 1944), 107–11.

"Butler's Boondoggles," *Newsweek*, XXII (December 27, 1943), 40–42.

Carter, Adam. "A Review of the Fourth Pan American Commercial Conference," *Bulletin of the Pan American Union*, LXV (December 1931), 1237–44.

Cleven, N. Andrew N. "Mr. Hoover Concludes Good-Will Mission in South America," *Current History*, XXIX (February 1929), 852–55.

————. "President-elect Hoover's Visit to South America," *ibid.*, XXIX (January 1929), 683–85.

Collings, Harry T. "Importance of Our Relations with Latin America," *Annals of the American Academy of Political and Social Science*, CLVI (July 1931), 133–35.

"Continuing Work of the Financial Conference," *Bulletin of the Pan American Union*, XL (June 1915), 747–48.

Cumberland, W. W. "Our Economic Policy Toward Latin America," *Annals of the American Academy of Political and Social Science*, CLVI (July 1930), 167–68.

Davis, N. H. "Wanted: A Consistent Latin American Policy," *Foreign Affairs*, IX (July 1931), 547–68.

Dennis, Lawrence. "Nicaragua; In Again, Out Again," *Foreign Affairs*, IX (April 1931), 496–500.

————. "Revolution, Recognition, and Intervention," *ibid.*, IX (January 1931), 204–21.

De Wilde, John C. "South American Conflicts: The Chaco and Leticia," *Foreign Policy Reports*, IX (May 24, 1933), 58–80.

Duggan, S. P. "Latin America, the League and the United States," *Foreign Affairs*, XII (January 1934), 281–93.

El excelentísimo señor Herbert Clark Hoover, presidente electo de los Estados Unidos de América visita el Perú 5 de diciembre de 1928. Lima, Peru, 1929.

"Final Act of the Pan American Commission on Customs Procedure and Port Formalities," *Bulletin of the Pan American Union*, LXIV (January 1930), 1–15.

"First Congress of the Pan American Institute of Geography and History," *ibid.*, LXVII (May 1933), 395–97.

Fisher, F. C. "The Arbitration of the Guatemalan-Honduran Boundary Dispute," *American Journal of International Law*, XXVII (July 1933), 403–27.

FLETCHER, HENRY P. "Quo Vadis Haiti?" *Foreign Affairs*, VIII (July 1930), 533–48.

GALARZA, ERNEST. "Debts, Dictatorship and Revolution in Bolivia and Peru," *Foreign Policy Reports*, VII (May 13, 1931), 101–18.

GARNER, JAMES W. "Recrudescence of the Monroe Doctrine," *Political Science Quarterly*, XLV (June 1930), 231–58.

GLOVER, IRVING L. "The Third Pan American Postal Congress," *Bulletin of the Pan American Union*, LXVI (March 1932), 169–71.

GRUENING, ERNEST. "The Issue in Haiti," *Foreign Affairs*, XI (January 1933), 279–89.

"Guarding the Health of the Americas," *Bulletin of the Pan American Union*, LXV (June 1931), 628–34.

GUTIÉRREZ, EDMUNDO. "Hoover-Yrigoyen-Leguía," *Aconcagua*, II (December 1928), 11–14.

HACKETT, C. W. "President-elect Hoover's Visit to Central America," *Current History*, XXIX (January 1929), 682.

HART, ALBERT B. "United States and Latin American Dictatorships," *Current History*, XXXI (January 1930), 744–46.

"International Conference of American States on Conciliation and Arbitration," *Bulletin of the Pan American Union*, LXIII (February 1929), 113.

JANE, CECIL. "The Question of Tacna-Arica," *Transactions of the Grotius Society*, XV (1929), 93–119.

JOHNSON, PYKE. "Inter-American Highways," *Bulletin of the Pan American Union*, LXIV (January 1930), 45–52.

"Making Effective the Conclusions of the Sixth International Conference of American States," *Bulletin of the Pan American Union*, LXIV (March 1930), 232–37.

MANGER, WILLIAM. "The Second Pan American Highway Congress," *Bulletin of the Pan American Union*, LXIII (November 1929), 1100–23.

MANN, LAWRENCE B. "Foreign Reactions to the American Tariff Act," *Foreign Policy Association Information Service*, VI (October 1, 1930), 261–78.

MARCOSSON, ISSAC F. "New Americas," *Saturday Evening Post*, CCIV (November 14, 1931), 3.

MASSIP, SALVADOR. "The Pan American Institute of Geography and History," *Bulletin of the Pan American Union*, LXIV (March 1930), 265–71.

MORTON, C. MANLY. "Hoover's Visit Builds Good Will," *Christian Century*, XLVIII (April 8, 1931), 486.

NEVINS, ALLAN. "President Hoover's Record," *Current History*, XXXVI (July 1932), 385–94.

NORTON, H. D. "New Avenues of Cultural Approach Between the Nations of America," *Bulletin of the Pan American Union*, LXVI (February 1932), 77–87.

OLIVEIRA LIMA, FLORA DE. "The First Conference of the Inter-American Commission of Women," *Bulletin of the Pan American Union*, LXIV (April 1930), 404–11.

"Pan American Conference on the Regulation of Automotive Traffic," *Bulletin of the Pan American Union*, LXIV (November 1930), 1095–104.

"Pan American Day, Its Origin and Purpose," Pan American Union, Washington, D.C., no date (mimeographed pamphlet).

"Pan American Day in Washington," *Bulletin of the Pan American Union*, LXV (May 1931), 458–69.

PHILLIPS, MATILDA. "Trade of the United States with Latin America in 1929," *Bulletin of the Pan American Union*, LXIV (April 1930), 414–15.

———. "United States Trade with Latin America—Calendar Year 1930," *ibid.*, LXV (May 1931), 511.

———. "United States Trade with Latin America in 1931," *ibid.*, LXVI (April 1932), 259–60.

———. "United States Trade with Latin America in 1932," *ibid.*, LXVII (July 1933), 565–66.

PLATT, RAYE R. "The Guatemala-Honduras Boundary Dispute," *Foreign Affairs*, VII (January 1929), 323–26.

"Postponement of the Seventh International Conference of American States," *Bulletin of the Pan American Union*, LXVI (June 1932), 388–89.

RIPPY, JAMES F. "The United States and Colombian Oil," *Foreign Policy Association Information Service*, V (April 3, 1929), 19–35.

SCHURZ, WILLIAM L. "The Chaco Dispute Between Bolivia and Paraguay," *Foreign Affairs*, VII (July 1929), 650–55.

SCOTT, JAMES B. "The Gradual and Progressive Codification of International Law," *Bulletin of the Pan American Union*, LXI (September 1927), 849–70.

———. "The Pan American Conference on Conciliation and Arbitration," *American Journal of International Law*, XXIII (January 1929), 143–52.

SCROGGS, WILLIAM O. "The American Investments in Latin America," *Foreign Affairs*, X (April 1932), 502–4.

SIMONDS, FRANK H. "Hoover South Americanus," *Review of Reviews*, LXXIX (February 1929), 60–70.

"Sixth Pan American Child Congress: Program," *Bulletin of the Pan American Union*, LXIV (May 1930), 461–63.

"The Sixth Pan-American Conference," *Foreign Policy Association Informa-*

tion Service, Part I, IV (April 1928), 50–58, Part II, IV (July 1928), 188–222.

STIMSON, HENRY L. "Bases of American Foreign Policy During the Past Four Years," *Foreign Affairs*, XI (April 1933), 383–96.

STONE, WILLIAM T. "The Pan-American Arbitration Treaty," *Foreign Policy Association Information Service*, V (November 13, 1929), 313–26.

STOWELL, ELLERY C. "Stewardship of Secretary Stimson," *American Journal of International Law*, XXVII (January 1933), 102–4.

STUART, GRAHAM H. *The Tacna-Arica Dispute*. World Peace Foundation Pamphlets, X (1927), No. 1.

SULLIVAN, MARK. "Hoover Economics," *Fortune*, VI (July 1932), 34–39.

———. "President Hoover in International Relations," *Yale Review*, XIX (December 1929), 219–32.

———. "With Hoover in Latin America," *Reviews of Reviews*, LXXIX (February 1929), 53–57.

THOMAS, DAVID Y. "The Monroe Doctrine from Roosevelt to Roosevelt," *The South Atlantic Quarterly*, XXXIV (April 1935), 117–36.

THOMSON, CHARLES A. "The Caribbean Situation: Nicaragua and Salvador," *Foreign Policy Reports*, IX (August 30, 1933), 142–48.

THURSTON, WALTER C. "Relations with Our Latin American Neighbors," *Annals of the American Academy of Political and Social Science*, CLVI (July 1931), 116–25.

WILHELM, DONALD. "Mr. Hoover as Secretary of Commerce," *World's Work*, XLIII (February 1922), 407–10.

WILLIAMS, SIR JOHN F. "Recognition," *Transactions of the Grotius Society*, XV (1929), 53–81.

WINKLER, MAX, AND W. W. CUMBERLAND. "Investments and National Policy of the United States in Latin America," *American Economic Review*, XXII (March 1932) supplement, 144–84.

WINKLER, MAX, AND MAXWELL S. STEWART. "Recent Defaults of Government Loans," *Foreign Policy Reports*, VII (January 6, 1932), 395–97.

WOOLSEY, LESTER H. "Boundary Disputes in Latin America," *American Journal of International Law*, XXV (April 1931), 324–33.

———. "The Chaco Dispute," *ibid.*, XXVI (October 1932), 796–801.

———. "Leticia Dispute Between Colombia and Peru," *ibid.*, XXVII (April 1933), 317–24, and XXVII (July 1933), 525–27.

———. "Recognition of the Government of El Salvador," *ibid.*, XXVIII (April 1934), 325–29.

———. "Shooting of Two Mexican Students," *ibid.*, XXV (July 1931), 514–16.

Woolsey, Lester H. "The Tacna-Arica Settlement," *ibid.*, XXIII (July 1929), 605–10.

Wright, Quincy. "The Stimson Note of January 7, 1932," *American Journal of International Law*, XXVI (April 1932), 342–48.

BOOKS

Aguirre Achá, José. *La antigua provincia de Chiquitos.* La Paz, Bolivia, 1933.

Bailey, Thomas A. *A Diplomatic History of the American People.* 2d ed. New York, 1945.

Baker, Ray S., and William E. Dodd, eds. *The Public Papers of Woodrow Wilson.* 2 vols. New York, 1926.

Barros, Jayme de. *Ocho años de política exterior del Brasil.* Rio de Janeiro, 1938.

Barros Arana, Diego. *Historia de la Guerra del Pacífico.* Santiago, Chile, 1914.

Beals, Carleton. *Banana Gold.* Philadelphia, 1932.

———. *The Crime of Cuba.* Philadelphia, 1934.

———. *Fire on the Andes.* Philadelphia, 1934.

Belaunde, Victor A. *The Treaty of Ancón in the Light of International Law.* Washington, D.C., (1922).

Bemis, Samuel F. *A Diplomatic History of the United States.* Rev. ed. New York, 1942.

———. *The Latin American Policy of the United States.* New York, 1943.

Bidwell, Percy W. *The Invisible Tariff.* New York, 1940.

Bryn-Jones, David. *Frank B. Kellogg: A Biography.* New York, 1937.

Cabeza de Vaca, Manuel. *La posición del Ecuador en el conflicto colombo-peruano.* Quito, Ecuador, 1934.

Callahan, James M. *American Foreign Policy in Mexican Relations.* New York, 1932.

Chapman, Charles E. *Republican Hispanic America.* New York, 1937.

Dávila, Carlos G. *North American Imperialism.* New York, 1930.

Dennis, William J. *Tacna and Arica: An Account of the Chile-Peru Boundary Dispute and of the Arbitrations by the United States.* New Haven, Conn., 1931.

Denny, Harold N. *Dollars for Bullets.* New York, 1929.

Dexter, Walter F. *Herbert Hoover and American Individualism.* New York, 1932.

Domínguez, Manuel. *Seven Kings and Ten Viceroys Affirm the Rights of Paraguay over the Chaco.* Washington, D.C., 1937.

DUNN, FREDERICK S. *The Diplomatic Protection of Americans in Mexico.* New York, 1933.

EMERSON, EDWIN. *Hoover and His Times.* Garden City, N.Y., 1932.

FEUERLEIN, WILLY, AND ELIZABETH HANNAN. *Dollars in Latin America.* New York, 1941.

FINOT, ENRIQUE. *The Chaco War and the United States.* New York, 1934.

FITZGIBBON, RUSSELL H. *Cuba and the United States, 1900–1935.* Menasha, Wis., 1935.

FREE, ARTHUR M. *Herbert Hoover.* Baltimore, 1929.

GARNER, JAMES W. *American Foreign Policies.* New York, 1928.

GIL, ENRIQUE. *La evolución del pan-americanismo.* Buenos Aires, 1932.

GUGGENHEIM, HARRY F. *The United States and Cuba.* New York, 1934.

HAMPTON, VERNON B. *Breasting World Frontiers: Herbert Hoover's Achievements.* Stapleton, N.Y., 1933.

HASLUCK, EUGENE L. *Foreign Affairs, 1919–1937.* New York, 1938.

HILL, HARRY W., ed. *President-elect Herbert Hoover's Good-Will Cruise to Central and South America: This Being a Log of the Trip Aboard the U.S.S. Maryland.* San Francisco, 1929.

HILL, LAWRENCE F. *Diplomatic Relations Between the United States and Brazil.* Durham, N.C., 1932.

HOOVER, HERBERT C. *Addresses upon the American Road.* New York, 1938.

——. *Campaign Speeches of 1932.* Garden City, N.Y., 1933.

——. *Hoover After Dinner.* New York, 1933.

——. *The New Day: Campaign Speeches of Herbert Hoover, 1928.* Stanford University, Calif., 1928.

HOWLAND, CHARLES P., ed. *Survey of American Foreign Relations, 1928–1931.* 4 vols. New Haven, Conn., 1928–1931.

HUGHES, CHARLES E. *Our Relations to the Nations of the Western Hemisphere.* Princeton, N.J., 1928.

HULL, CORDELL. *The Memoirs of Cordell Hull.* 2 vols. New York, 1948.

IRELAND, GORDON. *Boundaries, Possessions, and Conflicts in Central and North America and the Caribbean.* Cambridge, Mass., 1941.

——. *Boundaries, Possessions, and Conflicts in South America.* Cambridge, Mass., 1938.

IRWIN, WILLIAM H. *Herbert Hoover: A Reminiscent Biography.* New York, 1928.

JESSUP, PHILIP C. *Elihu Root.* 2 vols. New York, 1938.

JONES, CHESTER L. *The Caribbean Since 1900.* New York, 1936.

——. *Guatemala Past and Present.* Minneapolis, 1940.

JOSLIN, THEODORE G. *Hoover off the Record.* Garden City, N.Y., 1934.

KENNEDY, HUGH A. S. *Hoover in 1932.* San Francisco, 1931.

KEPNER, CHARLES D., JR., AND JAY H. SOOTHILL. *The Banana Empire.* New York, 1935.

LARKIN, JOHN D. *The President's Control of the Tariff.* Cambridge, Mass., 1936.

LAUTERPACHT, H. *Recognition in International Law.* Cambridge, Mass., 1947.

LIPPMAN, WALTER, AND WILLIAM O. SCROGGS, eds. *The United States in World Affairs, 1931–1933.* 3 vols. New York, 1932–1934.

LIPSCOMB, ANDREW A., ed. *The Writings of Thomas Jefferson.* 20 vols. Washington, D.C., 1903–1904.

LOZA, LÉON M. *El laudo Hayes.* La Paz, Bolivia, 1936.

LYONS, EUGENE. *Our Unknown Ex-President.* Garden City, N.Y., 1948.

McCAIN, WILLIAM D. *The United States and the Republic of Panama.* Durham, N.C., 1937.

McCORKLE, STUART A. *American Policy of Recognition Towards Mexico.* Baltimore, 1933.

McMAHON, JOHN L. *Recent Changes in the Recognition Policy of the United States.* Washington, D.C., 1933.

MARTÍNEZ LÓPEZ, EDUARDO. *Honduras y Guatemala: Límites.* Tegucigalpa, Honduras, 1928.

MEJÍA ROBLEDO, ALFONSO. *Los piratas del amazonas.* Panama, 1933.

MILLINGTON, HERBERT. *American Diplomacy and the War of the Pacific.* New York, 1948.

MILLSPAUGH, ARTHUR C. *Haiti Under American Control, 1915–1930.* Boston, 1931.

MONTAGUE, LUDWELL L. *Haiti and the United States, 1714–1938.* Durham, N.C., 1940.

MUNRO, DANA G. *The United States and the Caribbean Area.* Boston, 1934.

MYERS, WILLIAM S. *The Foreign Policies of Herbert Hoover.* New York, 1940.

MYERS, WILLIAM S., ed. *The State Papers and Other Public Writings of Herbert Hoover.* 2 vols. Garden City, N.Y., 1934.

MYERS, WILLIAM S., AND WALTER H. NEWTON. *The Hoover Administration.* New York, 1936.

NERVAL, GASTON. *Autopsy of the Monroe Doctrine.* New York, 1934.

NEUMANN, WILLIAM L., JR. *Recognition of Governments in the Americas.* Washington, D.C., 1947.

NICOLSON, HAROLD. *Dwight Morrow.* New York, 1935.

PALACIOS, ALFREDO L. *Nuestra América y el imperialismo yanqui.* Madrid, 1930.

PARKS, E. TAYLOR. *Colombia and the United States, 1765–1934.* Durham, N.C., 1935.

PERKINS, DEXTER. *Hands Off: A History of the Monroe Doctrine.* Boston, 1941.

———. *The United States and the Caribbean.* Cambridge, Mass., 1947.

PORTES GIL, EMILIO. *Quince años de política mexicana.* Mexico City, 1941.

REYNOLDS, THOMAS HARRISON, ed. *As Our Neighbors See Us.* Stillwater, Okla., 1940.

RIPPY, JAMES F. *The Capitalists and Colombia.* New York, 1931.

ROBINSON, EDGAR E. *The Presidential Vote, 1898–1932.* Stanford University, Calif., 1934.

ROIG DE LEUCHSEURING, EMILIO. *El intervencionismo, mal de males de Cuba republicana.* San José, Costa Rica, 1931.

ROOSEVELT, THEODORE, JR. *Colonial Policies of the United States.* New York, 1937.

SÁENZ, ALFREDO. *La situación bananera en los países del Caribe.* San José, Costa Rica, 1928.

SALIN, JEAN. *L'évolution du contrôle des Etats-Unis en Amérique Centrale et Caraïbe.* Lyon, France, 1937.

SAN CRISTÓVAL, EVARISTO. *Páginas internacionales.* Lima, Peru, 1932.

SCOTT, JAMES B., ed. *The International Conferences of American States, 1889–1928.* New York, 1931.

SEARS, LOUIS M. *History of American Foreign Relations.* 2d ed. New York, 1935.

SHEPARDSON, WHITNEY H., AND WILLIAM O. SCROGGS, eds. *The United States in World Affairs, 1934–1935.* 2 vols. New York, 1935–1936.

STIMSON, HENRY L. *American Policy in Nicaragua.* New York, 1927.

STIMSON, HENRY L., AND MCGEORGE BUNDY. *On Active Service in Peace and War.* New York, 1948.

STRODE, HUDSON. *The Pageant of Cuba.* New York, 1934.

STUART, GRAHAM H. *American Diplomatic and Consular Practice.* New York, 1936.

———. *The Department of State.* New York, 1949.

———. *Latin America and the United States.* 4th ed. New York, 1943.

TESSAN, FRANÇOIS DE. *Le président Hoover et la politique américaine.* Paris (1931).

Toynbee, Arnold J. *Survey of International Affairs, 1920–1938.* 16 vols. London, 1925–1941.

Uribe, José Antonio. *Colombia y el Perú.* Bogotá, Colombia, 1931.

Wambaugh, Sarah. *Plebiscites Since the World War.* 2 vols. Washington, D.C., 1933.

Welles, Sumner. *The Time for Decision.* New York, 1944.

Whitaker, Arthur P. *The United States and the Independence of Latin America.* Baltimore, 1941.

Wilbur, Ray Lyman, and Arthur M. Hyde. *The Hoover Policies.* New York, 1937.

Yepes, Jesús M. *Le panaméricanisme au point de vue historique, juridique et politique.* Paris, 1936.

HANDBOOKS AND ENCYCLOPEDIAS

Council on Foreign Relations. *Political Handbook of the World.* New Haven, Conn., 1927– (annual publication).

Hackworth, Green H. *Digest of International Law.* 8 vols. Washington, D.C., 1940.

Moore, John B. *A Digest of International Law.* 8 vols. Washington, D.C., 1906.

Vizetelly, Frank H., ed. *The New International Yearbook, 1932–1933.* 2 vols. New York, 1933–1934.

Wade, Herbert T., ed. *The New International Yearbook, 1928–1931.* 4 vols. New York, 1929–1932.

Yust, Walter, ed. *Encyclopaedia Britannica.* 24 vols. Chicago, 1943.

INDEX

Agriculture, 117

Airplane service: supported by Hoover, 120; inauguration of, between United States and Latin America, 121

Amapala, Honduras, scene of Hoover's first speech on trip, 40

Amazon River, scene of hostilities, 40

Ancón, Treaty of, 25

Apristas in Leticia, 40–41

Araujo, Arturo, President of Salvador, 57

Arbitration, see Chaco, Conciliation, Guatemala, Honduras, Leticia, Tacna-Arica

Argentina: attacks United States tariff at Havana (1928), 11; cool reception of Hoover, 20; boundary dispute with Paraguay, 35; attempts reconciliation between Bolivia and Paraguay, 36; protests to Japan over newspaper article, 47; opposes Monroe Doctrine, 47 n.; antiwar pact an attack on intervention, 60; opposes Smoot-Hawley tariff, 76; leading United States customer in Latin America, 77; Sandino seeks support of, 80; revolution in (1930), 92; sends scholars and teachers to United States, 114

Army engineers, United States, survey Nicaraguan canal route, 84

Art, inter-American exhibit of, 118

Asiatic Monroe Doctrine, 47; see also Monroe Doctrine

Automotive Traffic, Pan-American Conference on the Regulation of, 117

Aux Cayes, Haiti, scene of anti–United States riot, 86

Bank of Mexico, sacked by rebels, 95

Barco concession (Colombia), 110

Barrett, John, Director General of Pan American Union, 14 n., 75 n.

Blaine, James G., Secretary of State, 118

Blockade, paper (Brazil, 1939), 100

Bolivia: excluded from Tacna-Arica settlement, 30; outlet to Pacific for, 30 n.; boundary conflict with Paraguay, 35–38; revolution in (1930), 37, 92; declares war on Paraguay, 38; see also Chaco, Tacna-Arica

Bolognesi (Peruvian cruiser), 44

Bomb plot against Hoover, 20, 20 n.

Boundary disputes, see Argentina, Chaco, Guatemala, Honduras, Leticia, Tacna-Arica

Brazil: objects to Salomón - Lozano Treaty, 39; offers solution for Leticia conflict, 42; revolution in (1930), 54, 98; embargo on foreign flour, 74; asks for United States arms embargo against insurgents, 98; proclaims paper blockade, 100; purchases planes from United States, 101

Briand, Aristide, French Foreign Minister, works to outlaw war, 7; *see also* Kellogg-Briand Pact

Bryan, William J., Secretary of State, 34

Bunge, Alejandro E., interviews Hoover, 113, 120

Butler, Senator Hugh A. (Nebraska): attacks good-neighbor policy, 125; quoted, 125 n.

Caffery, Jefferson, sent on special mission to El Salvador, 57

Calles, Plutarco Elias, President of Mexico, attitude toward land and petroleum laws, 8–9

Canal in Nicaragua, United States rights to, 84; *see also* Panama Canal

Caribbean, dominated by United States, 46

Carvalho, Daniel de, newspaper correspondent, 14 n.

Castle, William R., Jr., Undersecretary of State: quoted, 51, 125; explains United States policy toward Cuba, 106

Central America: Conference on Central American Affairs, 5, 32; dominated by United States, 46; recognition policy followed by, 55; General Treaty of Peace and Amity, 55–56; nonintervention policy of United States in, 65 (*see also* Intervention, *and under individual countries*)

Central American Federation, 31

Chaco: dispute between Bolivia and Paraguay, 35–38; Hoover-Stimson doctrine invoked, 37–38; League of Nations offers aid, 38

145

Date D